Voices From Behind the Mask

Remembering How We Felt As the Lockdown Began

Ban Mittal, Ph.D.

Voices From Behind the Mask

Remembering How We Felt As the
Lockdown Began

Ban Mittal, Ph.D.

ISBN-13: 978-1-7359839-8-1

0 9 8 7 6 5 4 3 2 1

www.OpenMentis.com

As the post-COVID world reopens and we enter the "new normal" world, we should use this experience to at least ask the question, *How should I rearrange my life to make it more fulfilling?*

No matter how irrational our ideologies, beliefs, and behaviors may look to each other, we share one common heritage: One nation. A modern, rational, and democratic nation. We can keep it so only if we do not fight a war among ourselves.

CONTENTS

V O I C E S

Preface

It happened on March 19, 2020. That day, the governor of California issued a statewide "stay-at-home" order. Within weeks most of the world was in lockdown. COVID-19 had turned our lives upside down. Across the globe, people faced the triple threat of contracting the virus, losing work, and losing freedom of movement. The lockdown meant we could not go out to stores, restaurants, even parks. And we had to stay away from strangers, even from friends. The pandemic had brought to all of us upheaval in personal, family, work, and social life. We had to rearrange our lives. For some, social distancing exacerbated loneliness and isolation. For some of us the lockdown had a silver lining—we thrived in the new ways of living. And we thought about our lives: What should life's purpose be? And how should we live the rest of our lives?

To find out how people felt at the height of the pandemic and braving the lockdown, in May 2020, I surveyed people across the USA. I asked them questions about their life during the lockdown and about their feelings, living that life. They wrote down their answers, in their own words—telling it like it is, pouring out their hearts, sometimes in colorful language. A hundred of those answers—"voices"—are presented in this book. Voices that are sad. And sour. And sweet. And soulful.

Among these voices, find your own!

* * *

As destiny would have it, on June 28, 2021, Australia declared a new lockdown to contain the new Delta variant. On July 28, 2021, the U.S. Centers for Disease Control and Prevention (CDC) issued new guidelines, advising all Americans to wear a mask indoors, even if vaccinated. Across the world, governments and public health agencies renewed calls for new lockdowns and vaccinations. Maybe you discovered this book soon after its publication, in late 2021, or maybe you are reading it in 2022 or 2025, it helps to read it with some psychological distance from the pandemic, well after we are out of the lockdown. As we enter the "new normal" world, we should use this experience to at least ask the question: *How should I rearrange my life to make it more fulfilling?*

When I myself re-read these 100 narratives—when I listen to these 100 voices—from each I find a thing or two to learn: something to avoid or abandon on the one hand; and, on the other, something to embrace and cultivate. In either case, from these voices I want to grow and enrich my own life and those of others whose paths I cross.

I invite you on this journey.

—Ban Mittal

THE
VOICES

Survey Questions

In the online survey, I asked people three questions:

Q1. How have you spent your free time so far? Did you undertake any new projects, activities, hobbies, etc.?

Q2. Has your experience of the coronavirus changed your perspective on life in any way?

Q3. Have you made or will you make any long-term changes in your life?

They wrote their answers—spoke their "voices." Some were brief and to the point. Some wanted to say more so they "spoke" more. I edited them as little as needed. So, herein you will get their original tone.

Q1 serves as a backdrop, so I place it near the bottom. Their answers to Q2 and Q3 express their feelings, so I place them at the top of the page.

Let us "listen" to the first five "voices" and then I will tell you a bit more about the rest of them.

Listening Session 1

VOICES

1 **2** **3** **4** **5**

The Prompt

Q. Has your experience of the coronavirus changed your perspective on life in any way?

Q. Have you made or will you make any long-term changes in your life?

Q. How have you spent your free time so far? Did you undertake any new projects, activities, hobbies, etc.?

Yes, it opened my eyes to how quickly life can change.

Yes, to slow down and take time to really ponder on everything in life.

(Jane, 56-65, master's, salesperson, $50-75K, MA)

Walking, yoga with Zoom, and reading to my children and helping them with lessons.

Yes, I appreciate nature, life, family, friends more than ever. I stay updated with relevant information.

Yes, I would eat healthier foods, exercise more, love more, communicate more and appreciate more.

(Ryan, 31-40, master's, finance, >$101K, GA)

I learned new hobbies, read books, used social media more, learned dance skills, learned to appreciate nature and life in general.

Yes, we lost freedoms this whole thing was a big hoax this is nothing but a government joke.

The only long-term thing I have in life was to protect more of my freedom.

(Chase, 56-65, college, business owner, >$100k, ND)

Went out drinking and socializing with friends more than ever.

My life will remain as it did prior to all of this. I was anti-social then. I will still be anti-social when it is all over. My wife and I are pretty private people and are a bit on the anti-social side.

This "Lockdown" hasn't really altered the way we were living before.

(Frank, 41-55, some college, truck drivers, $51-70K, VA)

I helped my wife remove cabinets and prep the wall for painting in order to build a new pantry in our kitchen.

My perspectives about most things have changed. The way I see life is different, something that has great value and yet no value.

I will try to lead the best life, help anytime I can, focus more on family and friends than on wealth. I will try to keep this feeling in me for a long-term change so it will become a habit and finally my lifestyle.

(Zach, 31-40, master's, senior manager, >$101K, CA)

I performed more hobbies and exercises and try to live in the most healthy way.

What Type Is Your Voice?

Did you notice how diverse the voices you just "heard" are? Such diversity exists whether we take a sample of people from across the globe or from within our own city or village.

To organize this diversity in my mind, I use a tool—I put the answers ("voices") into one of the four categories:

Sad. People with this perspective are suffering—either themselves or they are sad from witnessing how others are suffering; or they are feeling helpless in the pandemic and under lockdown conditions. More broadly, they are feeling dismayed just to see the current state of the world.

Sour. These people are unhappy with the restrictions placed on them by the new circumstances or by those in power. They resent loss of control. Or they are resentful of those who are not cooperating toward improving the current state or helping the world get out of its current crisis.

Sweet. The threat of the virus has made them realize how fragile life is. So, they want to rearrange their life's priorities. Also, the lockdown freed their time from many routine activities, and they realized those activities were unnecessary anyway. They now desire a better work-life balance and seek to spend more time on things they love or they think matter more. They are "retuning" their minds. For them, the lockdown had a silver lining, a "sweet" realization, or a blessing in disguise, so to speak. It was a wake-up moment that has energized them, going forward, to make their lives more blissful.

Soulful. The most direct meaning of *soulful* is "expressing deep feeling or emotion." Often, that emotion is associated with sorrow but it can also serve as inspiration to emerge out of that sorrow. It also has overtones of spirituality. Here, I borrow this word and strip it of its undertones of sorrow, but I retain its spirituality element.

I define its central content through synonyms offered by the thesaurus: "meaningful" and "purposeful." Thus, soulful perspectives seek meaning and purpose in life and they define their purpose in non-material (i.e., spiritual) terms. They cast their eyes beyond selfish gains and embrace the good of the world at large.

Now try to sort the next 10 voices into these four groups. Some voices may belong to more than one group. For those, you may mark more than one group. You could even use a stronger or a solid check mark and a weaker or broken-line check mark to show to which group a voice belongs more or less closely.

Some voices may seem to belong to none of the four groups. You may mark it as "other." Try to use this option sparingly. As much as possible, try to mark each voice *sad, sour, sweet,* or *soulful.* Go ahead, "listen" to the next 10 "voices" now.

○ Sad   ○ Sour   ○ Sweet   ○ Soulful

Listening Session 2

VOICES

6   7   8   9   10

11   12   13   14   15

Everything seems to go by so slow now. Everything feels the same yet so different, and I don't know how to handle most of it. I've just been trying to occupy my time with more of what I already did, and some new-found interests.

I feel that now since I'm staying at home, I've realized a bit more about myself. For starters I have a bit of excess weight that I want gone, so I'm probably gonna try to take up regular trips to the gym when I get out, for now though I'll try working out at home.

(Amanda, 31-40, high school, cashier, $31-50K, PA)

○ Sad   ○ Sour   ○ Sweet   ○ Soulful

> **Activities.** I recently took up drawing. I always liked drawing, just didn't have the time for it with work and what not, but now I have a bit more time on my hands so why not pick up the pencil and paper again?

It has made me dislike people even more. I will still have more hate for the general population, even if things were to return to normal.

Going forward: I really do not know at this time. I do not know what to expect in the coming months and how my daily life will be.

(Jason, 25-30, high school, manager, $10-30K, CA)

○ Sad   ○ Sour   ○ Sweet   ○ Soulful

I began learning ham radio communications and exercising more on my free time.

Yes, it has changed my life; never been in this type of situation in my 40 years of living. At first it seemed surreal... then my anxiety went thru the roof! But my relationship with GOD IS SO CONSISTENT... I realized that He blessed me—the bigger picture...so my mind relaxed while still taking safety precautions. I chose FAITH OVER FEAR. HE HAS THE LAST SAY!

Going forward: Yes, definitely... I will pray even more, all other things I pray about will fall in its place.

(Sarah, 31-40, high school, worker, <$10K, LA)

○ Sad   ○ Sour   ○ Sweet   ○ Soulful

> Praying, stretching, meditating, taking walks, doing home remedies to prevent our household from getting sick, quarantined by only letting a couple outside people in, watching the news @Internet

I think I took for granted the things I can do in this city. The restaurants, the access to the lake, etc... I will be doing more things outside of my home.

I don't think I would change much but definitely making me reconsider what happiness is like and that life is short.

(Frank, 41-55, college, manager, $71-100K, IL)

○ Sad   ○ Sour   ○ Sweet   ○ Soulful

I have mostly been watching tv and taking walks when possible.

I will try to be more of a person that people in my community can rely on in these kinds of times.

(Dawn, 31-40, college, administrator, $31-45K, OH)

○ Sad   ○ Sour   ○ Sweet   ○ Soulful

Sitting out on my porch, having reflection time.

Yes, I value my family and friends more. I hate the pandemic that kills lots of people but at the same time I am thankful I was given a chance to sleep, wake up late, next to my family. We argue more, talk more and LAUGH MORE.

I made plans all of my life till now, but now, I am just going to live LIFE ONE DAY at a time. Enjoying one day at the time and worry about later, tomorrow. I will treat my TODAY LIFE as if I would die tomorrow.

(Lisa, 41-55, college degree, sales, $51-70K, CA)

○ Sad   ○ Sour   ○ Sweet   ○ Soulful

Catching up with my sleep, watching dramas, trying new recipes.

Overhyped toxic vaccine propaganda not falling for the Corona Bologna. The mainstream media and the evil government using crisis to drive down markets so things can be bought back cheap even the sound of social distancing mental insanity they always making new flu 2.0 in lab it's only a test to get reaction evil will get their karma.

(Maddy, 31-40, master's, owner, >$100K, CA)

○ Sad   ○ Sour   ○ Sweet   ○ Soulful

Learned new skills. Everybody should know CPR! Statistically, you are most likely to perform it on somebody that you know or love.

Yes. I'm much more thankful for the things that I have. During these times when so many people have been affected by the pandemic, whether it be loss of employment or just day to day struggles, I'm thankful that I have my health and that I'm still employed.

Yes. This pandemic has set off many long-term changes that I plan to do. For example, I will be cutting back on my spending and start saving more money just in case something like this comes back around.

(Brandon, 41-55, some college, pharmacist, >$100K, KY)

○ Sad   ○ Sour   ○ Sweet   ○ Soulful

I spent the majority of my free time relaxing. I've watched much more television than I normally do. I've caught up on shows and discovered a few new shows. Also I've spent a decent amount of time catching up with friends over social media. I also FaceTime, Skype or do Zoom meetings with my friends and family.

No, I will never look at life the same post coronavirus again reason being is because the world will never be the same. It is a changing factor for everyone.

Everything in life is long-term changes at this point. I don't have a clue, the unknown is always scary.

(Maria, 31-40, high school, customer service, $10-30K, TX)

○ Sad   ○ Sour   ○ Sweet   ○ Soulful

I spent most of my time listening to music, playing my games on my cell phone, doing homework with my son, spending quality time with him, cooking for my husband, and just thinking.

I could be wrong but I think this is just the beginning and we in the US did not handle it well at all, so, yea, the way I look at things has changed. At a state and local level, we need a more comprehensive handle on things because you cannot count on the federal level any more, and least not NOW and we need to THINK about who we elect. I knew this man in the oval was wrong for the job....but if people cannot see from THIS DEBACLE he has no clue how to run a country, then we are in trouble as a people and a country.

(Alesha, 56-65, master's, director, >$100K, TX)

○ Sad   ○ Sour   ○ Sweet   ○ Soulful

I watch the news and TV shows (all day in the background, while working or relaxing) I relax by reading, playing with my son, shopping, or playing a game online. I am starting a LARGE container garden, and laying out plans for a new website I want to start.

Thinking of the Person Behind the Voice

Did you find that some voices were easy to assign? As I re-read them, I too was able to assign some of them easily. #7 fell easily into *Sour*. #11 also was easy to assign—I marked it *Sweet*. The pandemic gave Lisa more time and the silver lining she saw is obvious. I placed #8 into Soulful. Sarah's roller-coaster of anxiety and then finding its relief in her relationship with God is almost magical. Then, #10 is a short one-liner, but it caught my attention as being rare in that Dawn is defining herself in terms of how she can make herself useful to the community. This level of non-materialism, this level of "spirituality" qualified her voice as *Soulful*. Finally, #14 was a challenge, as it had some elements of *Sweet*, in that Maria recognized the need to rearrange life ("never look at life the same") but her cluelessness and seeing the unknown as "scary" made me finally mark it as *Sad*.

You don't have to agree with my grouping above. In some cases, any two readers are likely to hear the same voice differently. When you are not sure, you could use a second opinion. Why not do the next session with a friend? Or with the members of your book club?

But remember, the goal is not just to assign these voices. The real value of listening to these "voices" is in learning to understand the feelings of the person writing those thoughts. So, let's pause a few seconds to reflect on each voice in its own right. Listen to the next ten "voices" in this way.

Listening Session 3

VOICES

16 17 18 19 20

21 22 23 24 25

Better to chill and stay the f*** away from others; so many people are out of control and won't shut it down.

(Going forward): (Stay) healthier at home; stay away; travel by car; don't shake the hands of the other people.

(Justin, 41-50, college, teacher, $71-100K, AZ)

○Sad   ○Sour   ○Sweet   ○Soulful

Reading, TV, and nothing else; we haven't done much; I am Pelotoning more.

My life has changed greatly because I enjoyed my time with my family and I now know how to show more of love.

I will try as much as possible to show much gratitude to everyone.

(Paul, 31-40, masters, financial advisor, >$100K, IL)

○ Sad ○ Sour ○ Sweet ○ Soulful

I spent my free time doing office work, exercise myself at my leisure.

No change; everything will stay the same. No plans whatsoever.

I will keep my life running the same way as before the virus.

(Rachel, 41-50, college degree, health aid, $31-50K, CT)

○ Sad   ○ Sour   ○ Sweet   ○ Soulful

TV, walking, visiting friends and generally spending more time with family.

Buy stuff and stock up. See family as often as you can. Wash hands more.

Yes, buy more foods and be ready for Round Two of this great stuff.

(Jennifer, 31-40, some college, $10-30K, IA)

○ Sad   ○ Sour   ○ Sweet   ○ Soulful

Bored, no class, no friends or family time. Not able to leave the house is sad.

Perspective Change? No, not much for me. Life goes on. This covid thing is not my dance. It's the 20-to-30-year olds that desired to wear the masks so they pushed the buttons to dance with masks.

I may wear a mask forever just to be safe. It's funny the plastic bags that were outlawed had a comeback when the stores had to supply them. This whole experience puts a new view on garments like burkas. It got misunderstood, stupid people thought it was a religious garment but I am sure it was created for something just like covid-19 to protect against.

(Brad, 56-65, college degree, landscape designer, >$100K, CA)

○ Sad   ○ Sour   ○ Sweet   ○ Soulful

I worked on my gardens, made some face masks required to go anywhere.

This virus has gotten me to the point where I'm scared to do anything in life to stay alive.

I will be more careful in life to make sure that my family and everything will be alright.

(Jeff, 31-40, college degree, driver, $51-70K, MO)

○ Sad　○ Sour　○ Sweet　○ Soulful

I spent it working on other projects. Like cooking more and being a better parent.

I will stress less. Try not worry about things I cannot change.

Try to move more. Eat better. Take better care of myself.

(Tara, 31-40, college degree, teacher, $31-50K, MI)

○ Sad   ○ Sour   ○ Sweet   ○ Soulful

Read, cook, and exercise. Doing more with my kids.

Yes. I am much more pessimistic about the economic future of the US and world. I am likely going to lose my job or have my pay severely cut. My firm may not survive.

I may have to find a new job or start a new career.

(Matthew, 25-30, master's, attorney, >$100K, DC)

○ Sad   ○ Sour   ○ Sweet   ○ Soulful

I watched television, read more, and looked at artwork.

Not really. I have always had this perspective of seeing the bright side of things, it has helped keep me stay sane.

Change going forward? I already have, establishing a homework schedule, it has been a huge help in staying organized.

(Stuart, 41-55, high school, construction, $10-30K, LA)

○ Sad   ○ Sour   ○ Sweet   ○ Soulful

I started a few new projects. One writing project and I started kicking around starting a Twitch streaming site and subsequent YouTube channel for the card game I play. I also watched some movies.

I am afraid I will have less respect for people I used to enjoy, but who now pride themselves to be a**h**** by refusing to wear a mask.

I do not plan on living my life in the long-term any differently than I did before the pandemic.

(Emma, 41-55, college degree, vice president, >100K, MI)

○ Sad   ○ Sour   ○ Sweet   ○ Soulful

Spent more time cleaning than usual. Was able to devote longer blocks of time to hobbies and walking the dog.

This Is Me. This Is Not Me!

How did you do? Did you find some voices interesting? A refreshing point of view? And then did you find one or two voices to be, sort of, 'blah'? Nothing remarkable in those voices, right? Well, that is reality. People here are not writing literary novels. They are not writing to impress us or entertain us. They are just expressing their feelings, just as they felt them. In this book, I did not want to select only the voices that made an interesting reading. I wanted to select a representative sample. Simple *voices* and richer *voices* alike. With equal curiosity for both.

Here is something else: When I was reading them, my mind was always asking, Can I myself relate to this voice? I found myself asking this even without trying. So, I naturally contemplated each *voice* more. I understood each voice more. Those that echoed my own feelings. But also those where I found myself to be of the opposite type. I added a tool to sort that out. I add that tool for the rest of the book. Now you have two tools to use. Listen to the next ten *voices*, keeping these tools in mind.

A New Tool

I can relate to this *voice*: ☐ A lot ☐ Somewhat

This *voice* is opposite to
my own outlook: ☐ Somewhat ☐ Totally

Listening Session 4

VOICES

26 27 28 29 30

31 32 33 34 35

Trust other people less and continue the social distancing thing but keep young to improve myself.

Keep exercising more and stay drinking a lot more water and spending more time with my kids.

(Dave, 31-40, college degree, broker, $71-100K, IL)

○ Sad   ○ Sour   ○ Sweet   ○ Soulful

I can relate to this *voice*:	☐ A lot	☐ Somewhat
This *voice* is opposite to my own outlook:	☐ Somewhat	☐ Totally

Mostly exercised more and played video games. Spent more time with my children.

The experience has changed my perspective about life entirely It made me understand how my family is important to me My beard has grown much, not able to shave them in my favorite barbing saloon.

I would make a long-term change of spending more quality time with my kids and reading more and praying more often.

(Billy, 41-55, master's, general manager, $71-100K, CA)

○ Sad   ○ Sour   ○ Sweet   ○ Soulful

| I can relate to this *voice*: | ☐ A lot | ☐ Somewhat |
| This *voice* is opposite to my own outlook: | ☐ Somewhat | ☐ Totally |

I spent my free time with the kids doing our favorite hobbies like playing games outside or playing video games to bond.

It has pissed me off even more and made me super anxious and depressed.

Gather more savings so that I can live the life that I want to live in the future.

(Peter, 25-34, college degree, analyst, $$31-50K, AR)

○ Sad   ○ Sour   ○ Sweet   ○ Soulful

I can relate to this *voice*:	☐ A lot	☐ Somewhat
This *voice* is opposite to my own outlook:	☐ Somewhat	☐ Totally

I watched Netflix during this stay-at-home order.

I am terrified of the economic destruction caused by the government's decision to shut down.

I need to invest more wisely because I feel that the government has destroyed the economy I predict that it will last for years.

(Charles, 25-30, master's, attorney, $71-100K, MI)

○ Sad   ○ Sour   ○ Sweet   ○ Soulful

I can relate to this *voice*:   ☐ A lot   ☐ Somewhat

This *voice* is opposite to
my own outlook: ☐ Somewhat   ☐ Totally

I've just been working and watching TV, I have not undertaken any new hobbies other than listening to podcasts.

Everything is different now—people are worse than before (& before was terrible) & nothing is even worth going out for.

What will I do differently in the future? I'm not sure, it's not something that I can call right now, we'll see.

(Jacob, 31-40, some college, free lancer, $10-30K, CA)

○ Sad   ○ Sour   ○ Sweet   ○ Soulful

| I can relate to this *voice*: | ☐ A lot | ☐ Somewhat |
| This *voice* is opposite to my own outlook: | ☐ Somewhat | ☐ Totally |

It really depends on the day, we've tried to keep our schedule as much as possible, which has been at least 70% effective.

I am more angry and resentful of the government for causing the COVID19 and creating our work to go into economic depression. I am going to have to rethink my whole life in order to get back on my feet financially and emotionally.

(Hannah, 41-55, some college, dog walker, <$10K, CA)

○ Sad   ○ Sour   ○ Sweet   ○ Soulful

I can relate to this *voice*:	☐ A lot	☐ Somewhat
This *voice* is opposite to my own outlook:	☐ Somewhat	☐ Totally

Just watching tv and spending time with my boyfriend and my dog.

I will appreciate family and get together soon more. Kind of enjoy your freedom more. Spending less and appreciating my home more. Save more and think twice before I buy something.

(Brandee, 56-65, college degree, RN, $71-100K, PA)

○ Sad   ○ Sour   ○ Sweet   ○ Soulful

| I can relate to this *voice*: | ☐ A lot | ☐ Somewhat |
| This *voice* is opposite to my own outlook: | ☐ Somewhat | ☐ Totally |

House spring cleaning. Did a lot more home cooking and baking.

It's going to change based on everything that has happened. The pandemic has thought us never to always rely on yourself or the community alone. You have to cater and care for everyone. And this has taught everyone a big lesson. When the pandemic is finally over, I have plans to do lots of things for the future to take good care of my family more.

(Charles, 41-55, master's, info tech, >$100K, TX)

○ Sad   ○ Sour   ○ Sweet   ○ Soulful

I can relate to this *voice*:	☐ A lot	☐ Somewhat
This *voice* is opposite to my own outlook:	☐ Somewhat	☐ Totally

I spend my free time playing video games or working out.

Feeling grateful for our immediate family having made it thru with only minor cases. Still terrified for my extended family and friends; more disappointed than ever at America's descent into a failed state territory.

(Caleb, 31-40, master's, consultant, >$100K, FL)

○ Sad   ○ Sour   ○ Sweet   ○ Soulful

I can relate to this *voice*:	☐ A lot	☐ Somewhat
This *voice* is opposite to my own outlook:	☐ Somewhat	☐ Totally

Lol I have a 4-year-old and a 3-year-old who no longer have a preschool or activities or friends they can visit. There is no free time.

I am more relaxed and calm overall and it helps to keep my mind off everything bad.

(Debra, 21-30, college degree, sales manager, $31-50K, NV)

○ Sad   ○ Sour   ○ Sweet   ○ Soulful

I can relate to this *voice*:	☐ A lot	☐ Somewhat
This *voice* is opposite to my own outlook:	☐ Somewhat	☐ Totally

I started baking and writing poems for free time since I have a lot.

Time for a Pause

Did you notice some of the voices are becoming too similar? Actually, that is logical. If we consider all of the people in the world, they all can't be entirely different from one another. There have to be at least a million people who will think alike, act alike. Or maybe even 10 million. That the voices of two people chosen at random are similar is in itself an interesting discovery. When I find this, I feel comfort. I feel comfort that no one is alone in his or her outlook toward life. No one is an island unto himself or herself!

Sometimes when I see that the voices are becoming repetitive, I feel like stopping. But then, the very next voice surprises me. I am so glad I did not stop. And what does not surprise me may surprise you. Listen to the next 15 voices and see how many hidden gems you encounter.

Listening Session 5

V O I C E S

36 37 38 39 40

41 42 43 44 45

46 47 48 49 50

Honestly, not much will change about my perspective on life. I don't love the industrialized world or the digital age like everyone else does and if anything, this crisis has only cemented my distrust of it. If anything, it's only going to make me more stubborn about wanting to go into stores and I want to live a more down-to-earth lifestyle.

(Jerry, 25-30, some college, restaurant worker, $21-30K, KY)

○ Sad ○ Sour ○ Sweet ○ Soulful

| I can relate to this *voice*: | ☐ A lot | ☐ Somewhat |
| This *voice* is opposite to my own outlook: | ☐ Somewhat | ☐ Totally |

Nothing new. I do draw, read, and play more video games than I did in the past.

I will keep sanitizing my house as well as wearing face masks and gloves. Will keep cooking our meals, will cut eating out in restaurants.

Will not be buying anything but necessities... Will not be traveling by airplane or boat. Will limit my travel to my backyard.

(Gayle, 41-55, high school, property manager, $31-50K, CA)

○ Sad   ○ Sour   ○ Sweet   ○ Soulful

I can relate to this *voice*:   ☐ A lot   ☐ Somewhat

This *voice* is opposite to my own outlook: ☐ Somewhat   ☐ Totally

Just watching TV. Exercising, I'm on social media, I'm online browsing, shopping online.

Yes, I became more to myself. Spending much time in solitude and meditation.

It would help me become more focused on whatever I set my mind to do.

(Brian, 41-55, master's, information office, >$100K, NY)

○ Sad   ○ Sour   ○ Sweet   ○ Soulful

I can relate to this *voice*: ☐ A lot   ☐ Somewhat

This *voice* is opposite to
my own outlook: ☐ Somewhat   ☐ Totally

I improved on my coding skill, trying to learn new technologies that apply to programming.

Not particularly. I just want to be a better person and member of the community.

Being a kinder person. Reflecting on my actions and words more.

(Blake, 31-40, some college, hospitality manager, $10-30K, CO)

○ Sad   ○ Sour   ○ Sweet   ○ Soulful

I can relate to this *voice*:   ☐ A lot   ☐ Somewhat

This *voice* is opposite to
my own outlook: ☐ Somewhat   ☐ Totally

Reading, listening to music, gardening and starting therapy by telephone.

No. The virus is overblown. The lockdown should have been lifted a long time ago.

No, I have not changed my life nor will I. This country needs to move forward.

(Max, 41-55, college degree, treasurer, >$100K, AL)

○ Sad   ○ Sour   ○ Sweet   ○ Soulful

I can relate to this *voice*:   ☐ A lot   ☐ Somewhat

This *voice* is opposite to
my own outlook: ☐ Somewhat   ☐ Totally

Played with my daughter. Socialized with friends. Exercised. Cooked more. Watched some new shows.

Definitely won't look at life the same way. So much has changed as I have a different orientation about life now. I'd seek to do more for people, be nicer and enjoy every moment of life I experience. I will pay more attention to my family, enjoying my hobbies and interests and definitely explore new things. We never know, everything can just get messed up in the twinkle of an eye without warning

I haven't made any long term changes in my life. But I have intentions of making long term changes in the long run, when all this is over.

41

(Kent, 31-40, master's. CEO, >$100K, FL)

○ Sad   ○ Sour   ○ Sweet   ○ Soulful

| I can relate to this *voice*: | ☐ A lot | ☐ Somewhat |
| This *voice* is opposite to my own outlook: | ☐ Somewhat | ☐ Totally |

In my free time I took piano lessons and online music classes. I also tried to gain acquaintance with some new knowledge like cartoon making and software/graphic design.

My faith has already grounded me in the reality that there are hardships in this life, and that we are a pilgrim people in this world. I will continue to walk by faith and with charity in my heart towards others.

No changes out of the response to the coronavirus outside of being extra vigilant against Federal Government overreach.

(Fred, 31-40, master's, deputy chief, $71-100K, LA)

○ Sad   ○ Sour   ○ Sweet   ○ Soulful

I can relate to this *voice*:	☐ A lot	☐ Somewhat
This *voice* is opposite to my own outlook:	☐ Somewhat	☐ Totally

With the less free time that I had, I tried to keep up with the hobbies I already had.

I hope to never have to work remotely again, and will value personal interaction more.

No long-term changes that I can think of at this time. Maybe retire a little earlier.

(Alex, 56-65, master's, high school teacher, >$100K, NY)

○ Sad   ○ Sour   ○ Sweet   ○ Soulful

I can relate to this *voice*:	☐ A lot	☐ Somewhat
This *voice* is opposite to my own outlook:	☐ Somewhat	☐ Totally

Preparing my vegetable garden, reading more.

Yes, it has changed my outlook on life. Time is short and you need to take each day as a gift.
Eat better and exercise more to enjoy life more and to live more and more and more.

(John, 56-65, master's, professor, >$100K, TX)

○ Sad   ○ Sour   ○ Sweet   ○ Soulful

I can relate to this *voice*:	☐ A lot	☐ Somewhat
This *voice* is opposite to my own outlook:	☐ Somewhat	☐ Totally

Spent on hobbies and working outside and helping cook and doing my duty.

I am going to be much more anti–social. I will be less approachable than before.

I may consider working from home via the Internet.

(Logan, 56-65, master's, educator, $71-100K, MN)

○ Sad   ○ Sour   ○ Sweet   ○ Soulful

I can relate to this *voice*:	☐ A lot	☐ Somewhat
This *voice* is opposite to my own outlook:	☐ Somewhat	☐ Totally

I spend a lot of time on the Internet searching for money-making opportunities.

My Outlook is already changed; I appreciate getting out and being free.
I would probably get out and try and live my life to the fullest.

(Jackie, 66+, college degree, director, $31-50K, NJ)

○ Sad   ○ Sour   ○ Sweet   ○ Soulful

I can relate to this *voice*: ☐ A lot   ☐ Somewhat

This *voice* is opposite to my own outlook: ☐ Somewhat   ☐ Totally

I've been doing a lot more cooking, baking, doing things to organize the house.

I will be more safety conscious (e.g., washing my hands more, staying at least 6 feet away from people), I am more grateful that I have not been laid off from my job. More appreciative for what I have (e.g., my health, my family).

I will save more money, develop an emergency plan, stock up on essential items (e.g., bottled water, dry foods, toilet paper), try to pay off my debts as much as possible, and put away more money for retirement.

(Brad, 41-55, college degree, data consultant, >$101K, CA)

○ Sad   ○ Sour   ○ Sweet   ○ Soulful

I can relate to this *voice*:	☐ A lot	☐ Somewhat
This *voice* is opposite to my own outlook:	☐ Somewhat	☐ Totally

Watching more TV, eating more comfort foods, cleaning up the apartment more, talking to my parents more.

I won't have much of a positive view to be honest.

I think I will move far away from people and start a little farm.

I would just have more alone time. Now I have no alone time because of my son being with me.

(Veronica, 25-30, high school, artist, <$10K, GA)

○ Sad   ○ Sour   ○ Sweet   ○ Soulful

I can relate to this *voice*:	☐ A lot	☐ Somewhat
This *voice* is opposite to my own outlook:	☐ Somewhat	☐ Totally

(Did not answer)

Yes, I've been bored and much more lonely—I miss going out

We could not celebrate our 30th anniversary—all plans were canceled—very disappointed. Now we have to decide how to make up for it.

(Lauren, 56-65, college degree, real estate, $31-50K, FL)

○ Sad   ○ Sour   ○ Sweet   ○ Soulful

I can relate to this *voice*:	☐ A lot	☐ Somewhat
This *voice* is opposite to my own outlook:	☐ Somewhat	☐ Totally

Watched more movies, binge watched tv shows, browsed the Internet.

I will be even more of a germ freak than I was. I always had hand sanitizer on me but now I will use it much more often. I will keep distance from people and use this as an excuse to keep others away from me.

I may leave my job and go work somewhere else, because life is short and I don't want to spend it being unhappy. Also, I want to go back to living in the country without neighbors being so close to me.

(Jill, 31-40, college, assembler, $31-50K, KY)

○ Sad   ○ Sour   ○ Sweet   ○ Soulful

I can relate to this *voice*: ☐ A lot   ☐ Somewhat

This *voice* is opposite to my own outlook: ☐ Somewhat   ☐ Totally

Painting furniture, reading, adult coloring books, journaling, listening to music.

Not Making Any Value Judgments

You have now "listened" to fifty "voices." And placed them into the four types: *Sad, Sour, Sweet,* and *Soulful.* Which type are you the happiest to read? Me? I like all four types equally. The *Sad* type of stories show real pain, inflicted by the pandemic and the lockdown. Many of you felt empathy, I am sure. Empathy is a good feeling. It helps us connect with other humans. Try to feel that empathy. And we need not limit our empathy to just the *Sad* types. Some of us may find ourselves reacting to the *Sour* types. But for these people, it is natural to feel bitter toward those they believe are not doing the right thing. Therefore, the "sour" voices too deserve our understanding. We are not making any value judgments. We are simply trying to understand how various people felt. If we can bring ourselves to not "feel sour" toward those whose voices are "sour," to that extent, we keep and savor the positive vibe in us. And bring that positive vibe even to the "sad" and the "sour"—precisely the people who need it more.

As for the *sweet* types and the *soulful* types, if we find something to copy from them, something to emulate, something to assimilate in our own lives, let us grab it.

Thus, lets us read the *sad* and the *sour* to bring our positive vibe to them. And let us read the *sweet* and the *soulful* to "steal" something good from them.

Let's "listen" to the next ten "voices" with that mindset.

Listening Session 6

VOICES

51 52 53 54 55

56 57 58 59 60

Cherish the little things like being able to eat out.

Spend more quality time at home with my family and not worry about the materialistic things.

(Brooke, 41-50, some college, administrator, >$100K, NY)

○ Sad   ○ Sour   ○ Sweet   ○ Soulful

I can relate to this *voice*:	☐ A lot	☐ Somewhat
This *voice* is opposite to my own outlook:	☐ Somewhat	☐ Totally

I started home-schooling my daughter because the schools and daycares are no longer open. I have also started doing more crafts and projects with her.

All good ready for sports and sports betting and fun and fun.

Produced more streams of income and such with affiliate marketing.

(Doug, 41-55, some college, sports handicapper, $31-50K, MO)

○ Sad   ○ Sour   ○ Sweet   ○ Soulful

I can relate to this *voice*:	☐ A lot	☐ Somewhat
This *voice* is opposite to my own outlook:	☐ Somewhat	☐ Totally

Played games watch hulu tv and amazon prime and so much more.

More disappointed in the human race and how willingly we are misled and willing to bow down to anything.

No, my life hasn't changed other than the fact that I will be even more misanthropic than before.

(Steve, 41-55, high school, mill worker, $31-50K, KY)

○ Sad   ○ Sour   ○ Sweet   ○ Soulful

I can relate to this *voice*:	☐ A lot	☐ Somewhat
This *voice* is opposite to my own outlook:	☐ Somewhat	☐ Totally

Drank while fishing at private pond. Spent time with girl-friend.

Just in the way that I am saving my money for retirement, saving my money to buy a house. Has made me more efficient in how I save my money for long-term planning.

(Dennis, 41-55, some college, sales manager, $31-50K, NY)

○ Sad   ○ Sour   ○ Sweet   ○ Soulful

I can relate to this *voice*:	☐ A lot	☐ Somewhat
This *voice* is opposite to my own outlook:	☐ Somewhat	☐ Totally

I watched more TV. Researched different stocks in my portfolio and initial creation of my Roth IRA.

Too early to tell. I certainly appreciate things more. Probably never look at things the same.

While some are sacrificing a lot to keep things going, others are proving there is no limit to selfishness.

(Travis, 66+, some college, retired, $31-50K, NM)

○ Sad   ○ Sour   ○ Sweet   ○ Soulful

I can relate to this *voice*:	☐ A lot	☐ Somewhat
This *voice* is opposite to my own outlook:	☐ Somewhat	☐ Totally

Yes. I am trying smoker cooking. Always wanted to do it. Easing my way in.

Perspective? The same, with the exception of being more aware of how horrible the democrats are.

No, I wouldn't make any long-term changes in my life.

Being bored and angry with our governor for trying to be the next Hitler.

(Patricia, 41-55, college degree, $51-70K, administrator, PA)

○ Sad   ○ Sour   ○ Sweet   ○ Soulful

I can relate to this *voice*:	☐ A lot	☐ Somewhat
This *voice* is opposite to my own outlook:	☐ Somewhat	☐ Totally

(Did not answer)

My Conversation with Patricia

Before moving on, let's chat with Patricia (Voice #56).

Patricia has a strong opinion about a class of people that make up about half of the political leaders and about half of our nation's population. Surely, she does not know all of them, so her statement relates to a few people she knows or knows of. Her speaking of all of the people in that class is merely a figure of speech, then, I would ask her. I would be sure also to tell her that there are just as many people on the other side who call Republicans horrible. They also do not know all of the Republicans, and they too group all Republicans in a camp based merely on the few that they know of or know about. This much truth Patricia will appreciate, I think.

My goal is not even to convince her of any point of view. I first want to reveal to her that I consider her opinions entirely understandable and that I hold her in good esteem. That I am enjoying talking to her, and that she can relax and feel comfortable in sharing her opinions with me.

I would like to understand the basis of her opinion of her state's governor. I will begin by asking her this question:

"When exactly did you come to liken the governor to Hitler, and do you remember what had happened just before that moment that made you view the governor in that way?"

"The governor had announced the stay-at-home order on March 16, 2020. Was it that day or a week later or two weeks later? Or was it only after May 4, when a state representative (who happened to be a Republican) called the governor a Nazi and you heard that statement in the news? In other words, did you form your opinion independently? Or you decided, instead, to follow the state representative hurriedly, without looking at all the facts that motivated the governor's decision to lock down?"

There were a few facts to consider, I would tell Patricia. The governors of 43 other states had also imposed stay-at-home orders, 19 of whom were Republicans. Were any of them also like Hitler? In fact, the only other governor likened to Hitler was the governor of Michigan. She is a Democrat, but no other Democratic governor has been called a Hitler. Why? Because no politician of either party in 41 of the 43 states had called their governors a Hitler or declared these lockdown orders unwarranted. Why was a call to "liberate the state" issued only for Michigan?

Patricia, I have other thoughts to share with you. Tom Wolf had been the governor of your state since 2015. If he were a ruthless dictator like Hitler, why did he wait six years to impose a lockdown or any other kind of mass restriction on people? In your state, the first case of COVID-19 was detected on March 6. By March 16, the number of infected cases had ballooned to 3,000+ and was rising exponentially. Despite the lockdown, the cases rose to 4,842 in March and to 40,920 in April. But then the infections began to be contained: In May, there were 26,163 cases, in June 14,579, in July, August, and September about 22,000 a month on average. In fairness, I must inform you that in October, the number of infections rose to a high of 49,060, and in November, as the lockdowns were relaxed and a spike was seen nationwide, Pennsylvania saw 135,587 cases. While the infections plummeted and spiked in alternate waves, one thing is certain: without the lockdown, the infection rate would have been many times more.

Seven states did not impose stay-at-home orders (Arkansas, Iowa, Nebraska, North Dakota, South Dakota, Utah, and Wyoming). Six of those seven are among the top ten in terms of the number of cases infected and the number of deaths per 100,000 population. The infection rates depend on several factors in addition to the presence or absence of stay-at-home orders. For example, how well the residents of the state follow the social distancing and masking practices. Also, people in densely populated cities like New York are likely to be infected more than, say, in the sparsely populated Niobrara Country in Wyoming. The infection rate also depends on how many people visited the state from other places and how many of them were infected, a fact highlighted by a sharp spike with 250,000 new cases in neighboring states after the Sturgis Motorcycle Rally in South Dakota. Despite all these factors, that stay-at-home orders will and did curtail the infection rate is as clear as daylight. The governors of 43 states, 19 of them Republicans, did their civic duty by imposing lockdowns when they felt that stay-at-home orders were needed to curtail rampant infections.

Sure, the lockdown hurts many businesses. Or at least it seems so. Suppose you keep your business open and, fearful of catching the infection, not enough customers come in; then you may not recover the fixed costs of running that business. Without the stay-at-home orders, you will open your business and run it for, say, six or 12 months, each day at a loss; or alternatively, you could close down your store for one or two or three months or as long as the lockdown lasts, and then open it fully sooner and run it at the normal customer traffic and profit levels. As a business owner, which option would you choose?

Patricia, you mentioned your occupation as "administrator."

Maybe you work at a school with 1,000 kids, or it is an organization with 1,000 employees. Suppose there was an incident and the drinking water in your building had become contaminated. You discovered it after everyone had drunk that water. Assume further that the water had bad bacteria that will sit alive in our stomachs for one week. To detect if they caused any damage to our bodies, we needed to be tested every day for seven days. There was medicine, but it needed to be determined based on the specific effects detected in daily individual testing. Furthermore, assume that the bacteria flourish in cold temperatures; therefore, no food or beverage could be ingested below room temperature (sorry, no ice cream!) and the air-conditioner should not be run, despite it being the middle of summer. You are the chief administrator, so what will you do? Impose these restrictions or not?

Is it true that, given this incident, employees in your organization should not eat food below room temperature? And not run the air-conditioner even at their homes, keep the room temperature at no less than 70 degrees? Whom will you ask? Will you ask the pastor or minister at your church? Will you ask your city council member or a state representative? Or will you instead ask your school nurse, your doctor-in-residence, or your local government's public health officials, and follow only what these professionals say? What if a politician called you a dictator? What if a parent or a family member who had not drunk that contaminated water rebelled against your room temperature guidelines to be followed at the homes of your employees or school kids? Would you walk back your order?

What if it were a centrally air-conditioned building with no thermostats for individual apartments? What if you yourself had not drunk that water and if you lived in that centrally air-conditioned building? Would you rebel against the imposed restrictions, or would you comply with them? The cooler room could aggravate the adverse effects of the contaminating bacteria and cause permanent damage to the infected person's stomach. This will happen only to one person out of the 1,000 who drank the contaminated water. Moreover, you don't know whether that one person who is likely to succumb to aggravated adverse effects even lives in your building. There is a probability that he does. Just to save that one person from such affliction, will you comply with the restriction, or resent it?

Whatever your answer, I will still uphold my esteem for you. As for me, I will gladly embrace that restriction. Because to me, this temporary loss of freedom is no worse than many other restrictions I have already followed. I cannot drive my car without insurance; I cannot walk into a store without shoes; I cannot ride my bike outside of the bike lanes on streets that have the bike lanes; I cannot walk with alcohol in hand in public places; I cannot run naked through town; I cannot throw my litter on the street; I cannot scream inside a store; I cannot blare my music speakers at night; I cannot jump the line at Disney World; I cannot fly my drone without a license; I cannot get my medicine without a doctor's prescription; I cannot access the power supply for my street and turn it off for everybody; I cannot stop people from getting on the public elevator that I am already in; I cannot keep a person from sitting next to me on the bus; I cannot ask the bus conductor to stop the bus right in front of my house; I cannot stand up and walk inside the plane when the seatbelt signs are on; I cannot smoke on the plane or inside the airport or in many public or office buildings; I cannot occupy the fourth empty chair at a restaurant table; I am not allowed to have a loud conversation inside a library; I am not allowed to withdraw more than $200 from an ATM; I must wear a uniform at work; I am not allowed to pee in a public pool.

My freedoms are not absolute. They never were. In no democratic country, ever. Not even the freedom of expression is absolute; I have it only as long as my expression does not harm you. My freedoms are designed for me to nurture my creativity, to pursue my happiness, but also in so doing live as a member of a civil society. Living as a member of civil society implies that exercising my freedom cannot harm any other member of my society. Not one person, not one member, not one living human.

My restrictions actually define my freedom; by showing me the boundaries, they reveal the wide-open spaces of my freedom inside those boundaries; those boundaries give my freedoms meaning, even dignity. I know I simply cannot do this and that therefore what I can do is worth doing. I cannot exercise my freedoms outside of those boundaries; therefore, inside those boundaries the freedoms I can exercise are worth cherishing. I am not allowed to go out today at all; therefore, being able to go out tomorrow will have more value for me. I cannot have access to marketplaces for a month or three months or six months; therefore, when the marketplaces open again, my degrees of joy after this long deprivation will be much higher. I am being asked to shelve my freedoms for the good of my neighbors, that makes my freedoms holier. The suspension of my freedoms is not forever, but only for a finite time, only as long as the crisis is upon us, only so as to thwart the crisis; this much I can see, this much I must understand. In their suspension now and their resumption later, I must prove myself worthy of those freedoms.

Yes, of course, I miss not being able to go to the stores and browse the aisles of clothes; or go to the barber to get my hair cut; or go to my favorite restaurants. However, a large number of people in the world outside the USA don't have a restaurant or a store within five or ten miles to go to; many do not have the money. About 40% of the world's people do not have access to the Internet. And 663 million people in the world do not have access to safe drinking water. My deprivations—not being able to go out—pale in comparison to the deprivations of these people who do not have access even to life's basic necessities.

Back to Governor Tom Wolf. The lockdown order the governor issued on March 16 was only for selected counties, and only for non-essential businesses. By March 30, the death toll in the state had risen to 74—that is, when the governor issued a statewide stay-at-home order. The governor is the head of the family with 12.8 million members. 74 members of the family had died, and the only way to minimize the chances of a few other members of his family dying was to impose certain restrictions on all members still alive. To keep as many of them alive as possible, what should the head of the family do? If you were the head of that family of 12.8 million people, what would you do?

I just realized I have been talking too long. Patricia has been listening with patience. We have each finished three cups of coffee. When we meet for our fourth cup tomorrow, I shall be all quiet. I want to hear Patricia's side, her point of view. I want to learn as well about her hobbies, and how she occupied her time during her stay-at-home days.

Your Turn

Sorry, my chat with Patricia became too long.

Since you were in on that conversation, what is your reaction?

Am I correct in my arguments?

What will be Patricia's reaction?

How will you carry on this conversation?

What do other members of your discussion group think?

If you have been reading it along with your friends or in your book club, this is a good time to share your thoughts on my conversation with Patricia.

_____

_____

_____

I have realized that life is too short to waste time not doing what I truly love. I will live every day to the fullest.

I have made some (changes). I started eating healthier and exercising.

(Kim, 31-40, some college, photographer, $31-50K, FL)

○ Sad   ○ Sour   ○ Sweet   ○ Soulful

I can relate to this *voice*:   □ A lot   □ Somewhat

This *voice* is opposite to
my own outlook: □ Somewhat   □ Totally

Working out. I started horseback riding again after having taken four years off.

I really like how my community has come to-gether to make sure everyone is taken care of. I think my outlook will be a little more positive.

This lockdown has made me more cautious when going outside; I will wash my hands even more and try to use germicides.

(Meg, 25-30, master's, accountant, $31-50K, IL)

○ Sad   ○ Sour   ○ Sweet   ○ Soulful

I can relate to this *voice*:	☐ A lot	☐ Somewhat
This *voice* is opposite to my own outlook:	☐ Somewhat	☐ Totally

I started doing more crafts and I read a lot more. I have also started to garden so I get to spend time outside.

Probably not because my mental health is worse so have no motivation to do anything

I am definitely even more disappointed in Americans as a whole. I'm absolutely appalled at the behavior of many people.

(Angela, 41-55, college degree, personal trainer, >$100K, NY)

○ Sad   ○ Sour   ○ Sweet   ○ Soulful

I can relate to this *voice*:	☐ A lot	☐ Somewhat
This *voice* is opposite to my own outlook:	☐ Somewhat	☐ Totally

I definitely want to travel more, just wish I could afford it.

Life is now different as we now know just a sickness could cripple the whole world. We thank God and the president for their good work to curtail the virus.

My outlook in general has completely changed as our lives are now the most important thing at the time of the pandemic.

Made more investments ... Yah made some long term changes to my life in the aspect of saving and more investment as this will help to cater more for the family with or without government support as one cannot tell if the government will continue to provide more to its citizens all the time.

(Eric, 31-40, master's, specialist, >$100K, GA)

○ Sad   ○ Sour   ○ Sweet   ○ Soulful

I can relate to this *voice*:	☐ A lot	☐ Somewhat
This *voice* is opposite to my own outlook:	☐ Somewhat	☐ Totally

Exercises to keep the body warm and family activities.

What Did You Do During the Lockdown?

So far, we have not said a thing about the activities—what people say they did during the lockdown. Here too the range is wide. Some said, of course, they did nothing new. Was it because they had to work as usual? Or because their housekeeping chores had actually increased? Or because doing nothing was their way of relaxing?

And among those who did do something new or extra, was it just more of what they had done before—an old hobby? Or was it, instead, a new activity? Those of us who did have more free time, did we spend it more productively, or were we clueless about how to spend it?

You will find four types of activities (apart from "did nothing new"):

1. Productive work, e.g., DIY projects around the house;

2. Creative activities and hobbies (old or new);

3. Passive entertainment (TV or video or social media); and

4. Busy with work or increased chores and, therefore, no free time.

Maybe we can learn something from reading what people did. In the next *listening* session, let's take note of people's *activities* also.

Listening Session 7

VOICES

61 62 63 64 65

66 67 68 69 70

Not much except I get to spend more time with my dogs.   I LOVE THEM SO MUCH!!!!

Change going forward? None that I know of. At least, I can NOT think of any at this particular time.

(Carrie, 66+, some college, business partner, $51-70K, WA)

○ Sad   ○ Sour   ○ Sweet   ○ Soulful

I can relate to this *voice*: ☐ A lot   ☐ Somewhat

This *voice* is opposite to
my own outlook: ☐ Somewhat   ☐ Totally

Cooking, reading, dancing to music, exercising and working out in the yard with my dogs as companions.

My outlook will certainly change. However, it's always constantly changing. I look forward to change.

I would have to look at the landscape of what's going on and what exactly the change is to understand if it's a valuable or dumb change to make at a certain time.

(Scott, 25-30, some college, sales leader, $51-70K, OH)

○ Sad   ○ Sour   ○ Sweet   ○ Soulful

| I can relate to this *voice*: | ☐ A lot | ☐ Somewhat |
| This *voice* is opposite to my own outlook: | ☐ Somewhat | ☐ Totally |

Developing myself becoming an avid reader. I read, listen to podcasts, engage in group zoom calls. Lots of wonderful development during a time like this.

I will stop complaining about going away from home to work. I will appreciate my office space away from home.

I will just appreciate the freedom of traveling and visiting family and friends.

(Maria, 41-55, college degree, accountant, $51-70K, CA)

○ Sad   ○ Sour   ○ Sweet   ○ Soulful

I can relate to this *voice*:	☐ A lot	☐ Somewhat
This *voice* is opposite to my own outlook:	☐ Somewhat	☐ Totally

I have no free time. I have a special needs kid that needs 24 hr. attention.

Honestly, I am SO much less stressed bc I don't have to sit in DC traffic several hours per day! The stressful point is my separation from my parents and brothers (and nieces & nephews) in NJ. When the restrictions lift, I will be able to hug them all.

Yes, I'm liking this "reading before bed" pattern. I'm also liking the fact I'm using food that's been in my freezer or on my shelves for way too long.

(Hope, 31-40, master's, analyst, $71-100K, VA)

○ Sad   ○ Sour   ○ Sweet   ○ Soulful

I can relate to this *voice*: ☐ A lot   ☐ Somewhat

This *voice* is opposite to my own outlook: ☐ Somewhat   ☐ Totally

I work every other week in the office, so on my off weeks, I made a To Do list to structure my days. I'd start with a workout on the Peloton, move to cooking a meal, doing one big chore each day (framing photos, planting my deck herbs, organizing a room), and then in the evening I continue reading a fantasy series.

I am disabled and the only amount I had time out was taken away too. Just made me depressed.

No, I have not. I will not be making any changes at all.

(Cathy, 41-50, college degree, disabled, $51-70K, CA)

○ Sad ○ Sour ○ Sweet ○ Soulful

| I can relate to this *voice*: | ☐ A lot | ☐ Somewhat |
| This *voice* is opposite to my own outlook: | ☐ Somewhat | ☐ Totally |

I relaxed, spent time with the cats, played on my phone, worked on a puzzle.

It actually improved my life. Between the federal unemployment and state I was able to pay off bills and, start saving.

We are considering buying a house and moving. I have started 401K for both of us and started continuing my education.

(Monica, 31-40, college degree, area manager, $31-50K, OH)

○ Sad   ○ Sour   ○ Sweet   ○ Soulful

I can relate to this *voice*:	☐ A lot	☐ Somewhat
This *voice* is opposite to my own outlook:	☐ Somewhat	☐ Totally

Worked on the house. Reconnected with my wife. Got healthy. It has been great.

I don't know if it [life] will ever be the same; this has really changed my outlook on life. I will always feel nervous in public. I will always be afraid of germs and disease. This will greatly affect how I operate in a public setting. So, if the lockdown was lifted today, I'd probably smoke a joint and watch TV.

I wouldn't take life for granted. I would be more aware of my surroundings and proper hygiene. I'd still stay to myself and do things more with my family and not worry so much about social events and concerts. I have become good at working from home and would probably keep doing so if possible.

(Tim, 31-40, college degree, owner, $51-70K, VA)

○ Sad ○ Sour ○ Sweet ○ Soulful

I can relate to this *voice*:	☐ A lot	☐ Somewhat
This *voice* is opposite to my own outlook:	☐ Somewhat	☐ Totally

I fished, hunted, played games, and watched movies, I exercise and do side jobs. I also raise chickens. I try to do things with my kids at least once a week and I get involved in recreation league sports for my kids and I love the water, I boat and jet-ski and I go swimming often.

I can't wait to get out of this house and take care of my family the best I can and make everyone else happy.

Just want to be able to take care of my family and I just can't seem to see past this mess right now.

(Ashley, 41-50, some college, manager, $31-50K, AL)

○ Sad   ○ Sour   ○ Sweet   ○ Soulful

I can relate to this *voice*:	☐ A lot	☐ Somewhat
This *voice* is opposite to my own outlook:	☐ Somewhat	☐ Totally

Just watching a lot of tv and sleeping until noon every day and all of this has to change very soon.

I have a greater awareness of my finances and where and how I spend my money. I believe that I will approach the lifting of the lockdown with that same greater awareness and be able to live with that in mind.

I have learned to live more simply during this time and also to plan much farther ahead in my grocery shopping and meal planning. For the most part, I have enjoyed both and will try to replicate that more simple life.

(Peggy, 31-40, college degree, event coordinator, $31-50K, IA)

○ Sad   ○ Sour   ○ Sweet   ○ Soulful

I can relate to this *voice*:	☐ A lot	☐ Somewhat
This *voice* is opposite to my own outlook:	☐ Somewhat	☐ Totally

Exercising outside, binge watching tv shows, meal planning & prep.

I will become more resolute in my cynicism as it pertains to authority and those in government we have wrongly empowered and trusted.

Getting to know family better. Reconnections with family have been refreshing and have bolstered my belief that my best days lay ahead of me.

(Brett, 41-55, college degree, owner, $71-100K, PA)

○ Sad   ○ Sour   ○ Sweet   ○ Soulful

I can relate to this *voice*:	☐ A lot	☐ Somewhat
This *voice* is opposite to my own outlook:	☐ Somewhat	☐ Totally

I spent time getting to know family better.

Do Our Activities Have A Meaning?

Do the activities people engaged in have any relationship with the perspective they reported? For example, consider the people who engaged in more new activities, especially new hobbies. Did their answers on perspective reveal a more positive vibe? More than the answers from those who worked as normal and did nothing new? Or who spent their free time in passive entertainment e.g., watching TV? Let's listen to the next voice set with this in mind.

Listening Session 8

VOICES

71　72　73　74　75

76　77　78　79　80

Yes, it has made me more compassionate, I've donated much more to charity organizations.

Yes, I would learn to be more hygienic and helpful to others and also save more for emergencies like this.

(Gary, 31-40, master's, CEO, >$100K, NY)

○ Sad   ○ Sour   ○ Sweet   ○ Soulful

| I can relate to this *voice*: | ☐ A lot | ☐ Somewhat |
| This *voice* is opposite to my own outlook: | ☐ Somewhat | ☐ Totally |

I used my free time for new projects, activities with my kids like playing video games and on new hobbies.

It helped me be more conscious and aware of politics and appreciation for state and federal government views, helped me find a job. I enjoyed after being laid off. Now I appreciate my new job that is very different and fun from the career I had in the medical field and now living in retirement with less stress on a daily basis. With new job in essential business, socialization increased due to work contacts and making new friends.

Appreciate good health, continue to foster close relationships with family members, be concerned for others around me and assist as necessary.

72

(Nancy, 56-65, college degree, teacher, $71-100K, PA)

○ Sad   ○ Sour   ○ Sweet   ○ Soulful

I can relate to this *voice*:	☐ A lot	☐ Somewhat
This *voice* is opposite to my own outlook:	☐ Somewhat	☐ Totally

Taking walks, shopping online, cooking more due to restaurants being closed, virtual contacts, tv watching, did a job search, learned new skills at my new job.

I think I have a slightly different outlook on things now, seeing the way people acted, they let panic and fear drive them. Too many people looked out for only themselves instead of looking out for others. I've always been one of those people to be prepared for just about anything, food supply, water, etc., but I hope people can come away acting differently from this.

Well, I'm hoping to stay prepared like I always have, stocked up on supplies. But I hope my other new habits become long-term as well like my working out and spending more time with the family.

(Miguel, 25-30, some college, self-employed, $$51-70K, TX)

○ Sad   ○ Sour   ○ Sweet   ○ Soulful

I can relate to this *voice*:   □ A lot   □ Somewhat

This *voice* is opposite to
my own outlook: □ Somewhat   □ Totally

> Me and my wife got back into working out full-time, I also was able to take on new projects and get a lot of the small things done around the house.

I used to work as an EMT so I always looked at life a little different.

Change going forward? I believe I already did this before the virus hit. Although, I do enjoy visiting seniors.

(Cameron, 41-55, college degree, EMT, >$100K, NY)

○ Sad   ○ Sour   ○ Sweet   ○ Soulful

| I can relate to this *voice*: | ☐ A lot | ☐ Somewhat |
| This *voice* is opposite to my own outlook: | ☐ Somewhat | ☐ Totally |

I did start shopping for about six more households. They were seniors and/or unable to get out during this time.

I will enjoy the simple things that I can do freely. I will go out more and make an effort to see friends and family more frequently.

I will really think about my retirement and what I will do.

(Laura, 56-65, college degree, educator, $51-70K, NJ)

○ Sad   ○ Sour   ○ Sweet   ○ Soulful

I can relate to this *voice*:	☐ A lot	☐ Somewhat
This *voice* is opposite to my own outlook:	☐ Somewhat	☐ Totally

I did lots of cleaning and organizing. I also threw out lots of stuff. I spend more time doing gardening.

I'll probably kill myself soon. If I were not a coward, I would do the world a huge favor and blow my head off. End it all. It seems so pointless lately. I'm broke, fat, and ugly. I have zero friends or family. I haven't even spoken to a real person in over a month. Why am I even alive?

Thinking about suicide, fantasies of how I would do it. Wish I had the courage.*

(Josh, 31-40, master's, restaurant server, $10 to 30K, OH)

○ Sad   ○ Sour   ○ Sweet   ○ Soulful

| I can relate to this *voice*: | ☐ A lot | ☐ Somewhat |
| This *voice* is opposite to my own outlook: | ☐ Somewhat | ☐ Totally |

(Did not answer)

*Upon receiving this survey, the author informed the survey administrator and also contacted local police. No further information was available.

Sorry to Interrupt

Sorry to interrupt, but I would like to say something to Josh right now.

Dear Josh:

First off, there are a lot of people in this world who are eager to speak to you. For starters, just dial 800-273-8255. That is National Suicide Prevention Lifeline. A counselor will listen to you, advise you, and arrange a support group for you.

Second, if you reach out to local charities and social agencies in your town, someone will help you to overcome your current financial situation. Many of my readers reading your story will be happy to help, I'm sure.

You are fat? That is entirely fixable—even just walking a mile a day and watching what you eat will help. I am not a fitness and nutrition expert, but it is a well-established scientific fact that avoiding junk food and exercising can help reduce body fat—in most people. As to "ugliness"—that is just in your mind. Real beauty lies in how good your heart is. Still, if it helps you, just Google "Ugly people who became successful." I did and one entry I found was "9 Famous Beauties that Used to be Ugly Ducklings and Became Idols for Millions" (on Brightside. me).

I have met people that you might relate to, and I want to tell you about them. During 2018-2019, just before the pandemic hit us, I traveled across the USA and talked to more than 500 strangers. I was researching what made people happy. (I tell their stories in the book *50 Faces of Happy*.) I met "Austin," 19, in New York City, sitting in a park with his dog. Austin (not his real name) had spent the last 15 years in various foster homes. Life in the foster homes was so horrible, he told me, that he ran away multiple times. Now 19, he was no longer a ward of the state. His parents had been in and out of jail all these years and now they were out of jail and Austin had reunited with his family. His parents had no jobs and no home. Together they lived in temporary shelters and Austin did odd gigs to earn money to help support the family. I was about to express my sympathy, but Austin did not want my sympathy.

While in foster homes, he had already earned his GED and had applied for college. His goal was to get a bachelor's degree, then a master's, and then a Ph.D. He had always been interested in history and he wanted to become a college professor in history, he told me. That much for optimism under adversity!

The second story I want to share with you, Josh, is about Svetlana, whom I met in Iowa Falls (she allowed me to use her real name in the *50 Faces* book). Svetlana came from Russia at age 6, adopted by an American family. The family treated her very badly so she ran away as soon as she turned 18. In college, she found a boyfriend, but the boyfriend abandoned her when she became a victim of an incident, which also had left her pregnant. The incident left her traumatized and she wanted to commit suicide. Having second thoughts, she decided to go to a hospital. There, she was diagnosed with schizophrenia. She had not worked since 2014 and lived on Medicare and Medicaid. Still, she managed to earn a GPA of 3.5 in college, while also raising a beautiful daughter. Now she wants to get a master's degree in social work. Why social work? Because she wants to help others like her. And her dream is to start a foundation and name it *A New Beginning*. "When I start earning," she told me, "I would keep half for myself and donate 50 percent."

I would like to recommend a few books to you, Josh. There are more than a dozen books on fighting anxiety; I found these four easy to read and follow:

How to Overcome Anxiety by Summersdale Publishing (2021) is an easy-to-read guide with topics ranging from the role of omega-3 fatty acids in diets to boost our nervous system and brainpower to "unfollow negativity on social media." One chapter reassures you that "It is OK not to be OK." Another nudges you to connect with others in similar situations. The last chapter tells you the benefits of seeking cognitive behavioral therapy. One sample tip: "Think, will it matter in five years? If not, then don't spend more than 5 minutes worrying about it."

30 Minute Therapy for Anxiety (2011) by Matthew McKay

and Troy DuFrene. This is a similar but nonredundant book. McKay is a professor in Berkley, California. The authors teach you mental and physical exercises that will train your mind out of anxiety.

Make Your Own Sunshine (2021) by Janice Dean. Dean is a meteorologist on Fox News. She was diagnosed with MS, and while in her doctor's office, she befriended a nurse. The nurse wrote her a note: "There will be loss, tragedy, and it will push us mentally, spiritually, and perhaps even physically but resilience is only developed through adversity." This became Dean's North Star. Dean does not offer any therapeutic or mind techniques to develop such resilience. Instead she offers stories of people who suffered, and yet in their suffering they found ways of engaging in selfless deeds (e.g., making bow ties for dogs waiting to be adopted). Find something to do for someone and you will find light in dark times.

In the same genre, in *Tattoos on the Heart* (2011), author Gregory Boyle, who founded and ran Homeboy Industries, a gang intervention program in Los Angeles, offers a pathway to fighting despair.

No matter how bleak the current situation looks to you right now, know that many others are suffering and feeling worse, and yet they are braving it. There will be resources available to help you but you have to decide to want to come out of your current feeling of dismay. One of the books listed above is bound to help. I urge you to read them all.

I sure hope we can get back to business, back to normal very soon! It's rather suspect that government officials are using it as a reason to seize power and make some serious changes that affect our freedoms.

Not really. I hope to work at home more often, and maybe take a look at preparing in other ways for another similar event.

(Ann, 41-55, some college, administrator, $71-100K, TX)

○ Sad   ○ Sour   ○ Sweet   ○ Soulful

I can relate to this *voice*:	☐ A lot	☐ Somewhat
This *voice* is opposite to my own outlook:	☐ Somewhat	☐ Totally

We did do some home improvement projects and read more. Focused on hobbies I already enjoyed. Still have plenty to explore and do!

I am more convinced that half the American population are sub-standard intellectually, and more than 80 percent are grossly inconsiderate.

Yes, I will pay MORE attention to sources of products I buy. I will prefer American, Canadian, or Western European goods and will boycott Asian goods. It is also my intention to encourage family and contacts to do the same and explain why this is a good plan.

(Ron, 66+, master's, consultant, >$100K, TN)

○ Sad   ○ Sour   ○ Sweet   ○ Soulful

| I can relate to this *voice*: | ☐ A lot | ☐ Somewhat |
| This *voice* is opposite to my own outlook: | ☐ Somewhat | ☐ Totally |

Chores and education of child; support and help you out of the 45th!

Yes, made me more aware of things and really respecting others; this is a crazy time we got going on and we don't know when this will end.

Going forward: Keep doing what I'm doing now and never change it because I been doing pretty good so far and I been very aware of my surroundings.

(Joe, 25-30, high school, warehouse, <$10K, CA)

○ Sad ○ Sour ○ Sweet ○ Soulful

I can relate to this *voice*:	☐ A lot	☐ Somewhat
This *voice* is opposite to my own outlook:	☐ Somewhat	☐ Totally

I just spend my free time reading books, nothing else.

I was already apprehensive and didn't like being physically near strangers so not much will change there.

No changes because I was already prioritizing saving.

(Shantell, 25-30, college degree, manager, $51-70K, IL)

○ Sad   ○ Sour   ○ Sweet   ○ Soulful

| I can relate to this *voice*: | ☐ A lot | ☐ Somewhat |
| This *voice* is opposite to my own outlook: | ☐ Somewhat | ☐ Totally |

I've been working on my baking skills and trying to get better at it.

What Will You Say to Them?

Okay, for the next set, let's assume an even deeper role. Imagine you met these people. What will you say to them? Think of something positive. Write it down. Remember, we have to be nice!

If I met this person, this is what I will say to them:

(Memo to myself: I have to be nice!)

....

....

....

Listening Session 9

VOICES

81 82 83 84 85

86 87 88 89 90

Well, I think everything jumped back in too fast. So, I am still at home. I have an 81-year-old mama and I am taking care of her. Don't want her to get sick. And this virus is serious.

As long as this virus is out here. I am going to be very careful and stay at home as much as I can. Until school starts back; I work for the school system.

(Denise, 56-65, high school, bus driver, $10-30K, NC)

○ Sad ○ Sour ○ Sweet ○ Soulful

I can relate to this *voice*:	☐ A lot	☐ Somewhat
This *voice* is opposite to my own outlook:	☐ Somewhat	☐ Totally

If I met this person, this is what I will say to them: (Memo to myself: I have to be nice!)

....

....

I paint so I am doing more paintings from my house. And that's good for me too. I relax when I am painting. I go outside sometimes to paint to get outside and enjoy God's creations.

More jaded and critical of the government and our health industry and with less patience for selfish and entitled people.

(Daisy, 31-40, some college, freelancer, <$10K, KY)

○ Sad   ○ Sour   ○ Sweet   ○ Soulful

I can relate to this *voice*:   ☐ A lot   ☐ Somewhat

This *voice* is opposite to
my own outlook: ☐ Somewhat   ☐ Totally

If I met this person, this is what I will say to them:
(Memo to myself: I have to be nice!)
....
....

Reading fantasy books, taking up quilting, and play more online games with friends.

I'd spend more time with my family The pandemic has also showed me how we're always on the move, not slowing to appreciate life. I plan to change on that note.

I'd exercise more daily and spend more time communicating with my wife and kids and also with my parents.

(Aron, 25-30, master's, IT manager, >$100K, CA)

○ Sad   ○ Sour   ○ Sweet   ○ Soulful

I can relate to this *voice*:   ☐ A lot   ☐ Somewhat

This *voice* is opposite to my own outlook: ☐ Somewhat   ☐ Totally

If I met this person, this is what I will say to them: (Memo to myself: I have to be nice!)

....

....

I take online courses and play more video games. I also spend family time and play with my kids more.

It's easier for me to get things done because I don't have to leave my house.

I wouldn't make any long-term changes in my life because there is nothing for me to change.

(Makaela, 25-30, college degree, influencer, <$10K, WI)

○ Sad   ○ Sour   ○ Sweet   ○ Soulful

| I can relate to this *voice*: | ☐ A lot | ☐ Somewhat |
| This *voice* is opposite to my own outlook: | ☐ Somewhat | ☐ Totally |

If I met this person, this is what I will say to them:
(Memo to myself: I have to be nice!)

....

....

I spent my free time making YouTube videos and social media like Instagram.

No change I would never change anything the government tries to tell me to do; always an agenda.

No, I would not change anything, and the government needs to stay the **** outta it.

(Philip, 41-55, some college, <$10K, AZ)

○ Sad   ○ Sour   ○ Sweet   ○ Soulful

I can relate to this *voice*:	☐ A lot	☐ Somewhat
This *voice* is opposite to my own outlook:	☐ Somewhat	☐ Totally

If I met this person, this is what I will say to them: (Memo to myself: I have to be nice!)

....

....

Watched tv and played games.

It has helped me realize what is truly important—the health and happiness of those I love... I firmly believe we are opening up far too soon. I do not plan to change my self-isolating and social distancing until its clear there is a working vaccine.

I have decided not to return to work and retire early.

(Amy, 41-55, College degree, server, $10-30K, AZ)

○ Sad ○ Sour ○ Sweet ○ Soulful

I can relate to this *voice*:	☐ A lot	☐ Somewhat
This *voice* is opposite to my own outlook:	☐ Somewhat	☐ Totally

If I met this person, this is what I will say to them: (Memo to myself: I have to be nice!)

....

....

I built an above-ground garden and caught up on sleep.

Retire Early?

Dear Amy:

You checked the age group 41-55. If you are closer to 41, then it is really early. If you are closer to 55, you have earned it—almost. In either case, if you can afford to retire, good for you.

You still got 25 to 40 or even 50 more years to live. (Life expectancy for women in the US was 80.5 years in 2020—down from 81.4 years in 2019!). What will you do for the 40+ years of post-retirement life?

Doing "nothing" is not an option: If you do absolutely nothing, you will get bored of doing nothing. And if you plan on passive leisure (e.g., watching TV 24/7), you will get bored of that too. No matter how large our appetite for leisure and recreation, we need a break from recreation too.

Many people find ways of occupying their post-retirement time. Travel, learning new hobbies (e.g., music, painting, etc.), exploring the world of arts, history, cultures through reading and visiting museums; volunteering; babysitting grandchildren; practicing spirituality—any number of such activities will bring you new joy. Just choose what you like. Only, don't say "nothing." And don't go into retirement without thinking and planning what you will do in your post-retirement life. Not knowing what to do will drive you insane. And also those around you.

But, first, why do you want to retire? Assuming, physically we are fit to work, why do we, any of us, want to retire, especially retire *early*?

We want to retire early because, for many of us, our jobs are boring, tedious. "My job is just a job," we say. And many jobs are. At the same time, in part they are tedious because that is how we have visualized them in our minds and that is how we have enacted them.

In my research, talking to 500+ strangers across the USA during 2018-2019, I came across many people who enjoyed their jobs. And I am not talking of people with well-paying managerial and professional jobs, although there were certainly many of those people as well whom I interviewed. I met many people in menial jobs, and some of them had a refreshing way of looking at what they did.

In Minneapolis, I met Jayden, who worked for the city government. His job was to remove fallen tree branches and dead birds from the power lines. He said this task was challenging because for each incident of a branch stuck or a dead bird trapped on the wire, he had to think how best to catch it and bring it down without dropping it on a person walking on the road below. Every completed task was a small victory of sorts.

I met Jorge, a janitor in Boise, Idaho, cleaning the sidewalk right outside of Form & Function Coffee Shop on Broad Street. He enjoyed his job because, he said, he was keeping his city beautiful. When people are walking on a street and they see how clean it is, it brings them joy, he said. If he finds a street that people have made dirty by carelessly throwing litter, restoring it to its normalcy becomes a mission. Often he takes "before" and "after" pictures and those pictures are part of his album of personal accomplishments.

TED speaker Simon Sinek gives an example of a motivated worker in what most will consider a routine, tedious job. Consider a bus driver. They sit the whole day in the driver's seat, and some of them mechanically open and close the door, do not make eye contact with the passengers boarding the bus, and barely respond to a departing passenger's "thank you." For eight to ten hours a day for the last ten or twenty or thirty years, they have done it like clockwork. Then there is this one driver, let's call him "Sammy." (I am paraphrasing Sinek's narrative.) Sammy recognizes many of his "regulars" and asks them where they are headed that day and what their plan of the day was and whether anything special was going on in their lives that day. Before every stop, he wonders quietly whether any new people would come in that day at that stop. When he sees new people, he tries to guess what their destinations and purposes of the trips might be. Most of all, he is enjoying the fact that he is helping these people reach their destinations. Can there be a nobler duty than to help our fellow citizens reach their destinations? With every trip, week, month, and year passing, he can keep updating his score of the total number of people he has thus helped. Has he reached one million yet? We can imagine easily what keeps him looking forward to every day of his work.

Yes, someday Sammy too will retire, of course. But *early* retirement it will not be!

It reminded me not to take life for granted—ed because we are never promised tomorrow. I am going to live more in the moment than worrying so much about the future.

Cleaning up after kids who didn't have to go to school due to the coronavirus.

(Chelsea, 31-40, some college, supervisor, $51-70K, GA)

○ Sad   ○ Sour   ○ Sweet   ○ Soulful

I can relate to this *voice*:	☐ A lot	☐ Somewhat
This *voice* is opposite to my own outlook:	☐ Somewhat	☐ Totally

If I met this person, this is what I will say to them: (Memo to myself: I have to be nice!)

....

....

I had less free time than normal because others had extra free time.

I am very sad for all of the people who have had a difficult time during this period. I have felt very blessed personally by the chance to catch up on some things. Before all of this life was far too hectic and stressful. This has allowed me to slow down and get things done with more balance in my life between work, home responsibilities, and free time. I am feeling a bit anxious about life returning to normal because it was so unbalanced.

I will be better aware of hand-washing and doing basic things to ward off germs.

(Paula, 41-55, college degree, teacher, >$100K, FL)

○ Sad ○ Sour ○ Sweet ○ Soulful

I can relate to this *voice*: □ A lot   □ Somewhat

This *voice* is opposite to
my own outlook: □ Somewhat   □ Totally

If I met this person, this is what I will say to them:
(Memo to myself: I have to be nice!)

....

....

I cleaned up the bushes in the front and back yard. I decorated the front and back yard.

Not really. I have always had a healthy respect for life in general and this just highlighted to me that every moment is a gift.

Yes. I only go to the store once a week and plan on keeping it that way.

(Susan, 41-55, college degree, teacher, $51-70K, TX)

○ Sad ○ Sour ○ Sweet ○ Soulful

I can relate to this *voice*: ☐ A lot   ☐ Somewhat

This *voice* is opposite to my own outlook: ☐ Somewhat ☐ Totally

If I met this person, this is what I will say to them:
(Memo to myself: I have to be nice!)

....

....

Home improvement projects. Gardening. Lawn care. Reading. Grilling.

I'm going to get a tattoo and get my nails done again, I hate not being able to do that right now, I used to get services done all the time.

I hope to get a new job, I wanted to before the virus, but it got put on hold due to the virus.

(Sue, 25-30, some college, store manager, $31-50K, WI)

○ Sad   ○ Sour   ○ Sweet   ○ Soulful

I can relate to this *voice*:	☐ A lot	☐ Somewhat
This *voice* is opposite to my own outlook:	☐ Somewhat	☐ Totally

If I met this person, this is what I will say to them: (Memo to myself: I have to be nice!)

....

....

Activities: Sat on Facebook all the time, pretty much my usual.

On Work-Life Balance

A number of voices have spoken of wanting to reorient their lives toward more work-life balance. For example:

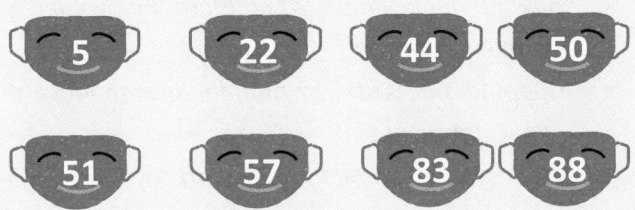

I want to share a few thoughts with them and with all of you who may also be wanting to pursue a greater work-life balance.

It is a good thing that the lockdown made you see what really matters and that you want to make some changes and live your future life differently.

Don't walk into the new economy, new post-lockdown world, with merely this generalized intention. Make it concrete. Identify five specific changes you will make in your personal life and in your work life.

To pursue work-life balance is inherently a good resolve but let us ponder why there is an imbalance to begin with.

Is it because you're working too many hours, sacrificing your family and personal time? If so, then you definitely need to find a job that will not overstretch you. In some cases, you may be able to reduce the need for overstretching by working more efficiently, by avoiding distractions, or by eliminating procedural excess from productive parts of your tasks.

Or is it because you don't like your job? If so, you need to find your way out of this rut. Any number of blogs will give you useful tips. For example:

- *How to Make Your Work More Enjoyable: 8 Tips* (Thriveworks.com)
- *Happiness at Work: 12 Simple Ways to Make It Happen* (Lifehack.org)
- *44 Easy Ways to Make Your Workday More Enjoyable* (theMuse.com)

Beyond all these tactical fixes, the core problem resides in the two-fold vision of work you have harbored in your head: One, you don't like what you do, and two, you don't see any meaning in it.

Let us take these one by one. If you don't like what you do, that's a basic problem and a big curse. We are going to spend the better part of our waking hours for 40 to 60 years of our lives doing something we do not enjoy! What kind of a life is that?

In contrast, consider the work we do enjoy such as the work entailed in our hobbies like gardening, cooking, embroidery, needlepoint, metalworking, etc. These activities are inherently relaxing, and many of them entail developing and mastering the skills of doing them well. Mastering a skill and seeing its outcome gives us a sense of accomplishment.

The second type of work we enjoy is voluntary work. We volunteer to coach a sports team, be a guest guide, or manage a ticket booth at a charity event, maintain the accounting books at a church, plant trees on Earth Day, work at a cleanup event in a city or on a highway, box groceries at a local food pantry, or serve food at a food kitchen. What makes this work interesting? Many of these activities are menial chores, yet we do them happily. Why? Because we see meaning in them.

The trick to finding enjoyable work then is two-fold: (1) Get good at that hobby, that voluntary work; hone on those skills; and (2) Find commercial organizations willing to pay for those skills.

Now let us reverse this sequence. Ask yourself this question: What if I were a volunteer at my present job and I were doing it without a salary? How will I enjoy it? How will I make it a hobby? If you draw a blank, then look for some activity you will like and also become good at—with or without pay.

Pay has nothing to do with the enjoyability of an activity. An activity that requires skill or mastery is enjoyable in itself. A musician enjoys making music; a painter enjoys painting; a carpenter enjoys giving pieces of wood interesting shapes; a mason enjoys laying bricks; a pilot enjoys flying; a barber enjoys cutting hair; a car mechanic enjoys fixing cars; a restaurant server enjoys serving food to a variety of customers. Or if they don't, they will not enjoy them, with or without pay.

There is nothing inherently boring about these jobs. Arranging musical notes to produce melody is a sweet challenge for the musician; for the painter, seeing colors on a canvas merge into an alluring image is a joy; for the carpenter, to shape a chair out of a tree trunk is an accomplishment; for a mason, to lay bricks in a symmetrical fashion is a skill to be proud of; for a hairstylist, to see the "before" and "after" transformation of a customer's hair/face is a small miracle; for the supermarket clerk, to see an assortment of groceries fit neatly into a shopping bag is an art form.

Yes, but when the same tasks get repeated, they get boring, you say. Is it? Could it be because we focus on the similarity but are blind to the diversity and variations in the repeat cycles of those tasks? Is all customers' hair the same? Are the styles they want the same? Are the smiles on their faces when they see them in the mirror the same? Are the arrays of groceries to be bagged for different customers the same? Do you have to put them in the bag in the same sequence, the same way? Have you looked at the shoppers' faces? Are those faces repetitive?

You see, we have defined our jobs as mechanical tasks performed on physical things: as food trays to be transported, groceries to be bagged, or hair to be cut. Not as the looks of different people to be modified with the haircut; not as hundreds of grocery shoppers to be sent home happy with their groceries skillfully arranged in bags. Not as different groups of diners who enter a restaurant—coworkers, families, friends, lovers—with different desires, different views of food, enacting their own different patterns of interactions. To watch what food they order and how they order it, to watch their faces as they take the first bite, or the last, to see the look of satiation on their faces, to "read" their nonverbal communications with other members of their groups, to watch all these mini-dramas, so to speak, can be immensely enjoyable. All it takes is a curious mind. All it takes is having an interest in humans as individuals.

What about assembly line work, you ask? Even in assembly-line work, it is possible to enjoy watching how a robot puts the parts together, for example, even watching it for the millionth time. Just wonder whether this one time, just this one time, the robot will make a mistake. Or whether the light falling on the finished product on the assembly line from a different angle will make it look more angular or more rounded. Will you be around to see this robot finish the 100,000th unit? When will that be? Might you wear a new outfit when you come to work that day??

So, you see, the avenues of seeing enjoyment in work are limited only by our imagination!

The second core element of jobs is their meaning—or the lack thereof. Does your job have a meaning? Are there jobs that are meaningful, and jobs that are not? Are there any jobs that are not meaningful? To answer that question, allow me to quote an excerpt from my own book:

> Sitting at your desk, you create a financial plan for a client's retirement security, draw an architectural diagram for a new stadium, or write code for the next killer app. In the factory, you install an airbag in a car, pour molten glass to make shatterproof phone screens, or weave microfiber to create athletic shirts that keep our bodies cool even in the blazing sun. In the field, you plow the land; in the city, you drive a bus for commuters; at school, you help a kid learn math; in the hospital, you inject a flu vaccine; in the diner, you cook dinner for starving guests; at the grocery store, you bag people's groceries. In these and all other manifestations of work, you are being valuable to so-

ciety. You are making the world go around.

I realize that I am able to work, eat, and play because all of the above jobs are getting done. Because you do your job. Each of the 7,877,066,000* humans lives because 7,877,065,999 other humans do their jobs. Our jobs are that important. Your job is that important!

(*World population as of July 4, 2019)

—From *50 Faces of Happy* (50FacesofHappy.com)

The purpose of seeking work-life balance, of appreciating life and friends and family, is to attain more happiness for yourself and for the people you care about. Now may be the right time, therefore, to ponder what true happiness is and how to achieve it. I urge you to listen to many good podcasts on this topic. There are three I especially recommend, no matter what your age, education, or occupation:

- Steve Jobs' Commencement Speech at Stanford University
- Denzel Washington's Commencement Speech at the University of Philadelphia
- Matthew McConaughey's podcast "Find Your Own Path"

(Find these on YouTube.)

This question of finding happiness is too important to dismiss lightly. If we just assume that we know the secret, that "I already know what makes me happy," we miss out on the opportunity of a higher level of happiness—happiness we are capable of finding, in and out of lockdown alike. To support your search for a well-considered answer, I recommend the following three books. The second and third books are light reading; the first book is not light and it energizes serious perspectives, but it is quite engaging, actually.

Think Like a Monk (2020) by Jay Shetty. In this book, Shetty, himself a monk once, contrasts our current mind ("monkey mind") to a "monk's mind." Monkey mind complains, compares, criticizes; it overthinks and procrastinates; it seeks short-term gratification; it is self-centered; it multi-tasks and bogs down in small things; and it lives for pleasure. In sharp contrast, the *monk mind* is compassionate and caring; seeks self-control and mastery; is disciplined; has clear visions and goals; and it lives for a meaning. The book translates some core wisdom of *Bhagavat Gita* and will help you transform from your monkey mind to a monk's mind. Don't worry, it doesn't make you a real monk, as in renouncing the world or living in the Himalayas. It gives you understanding and purpose.

Do Nothing by Celeste Headlee: Its title is tongue-in-cheek, of course, for it does not tell us to become a sloth. Instead it teaches us to break away from a life of overworking and overdoing and underliving. In nine short ("analysis") chapters, it first forces us to confront our demons—our current habits of working and overthinking. And then, in six short ("action") chapters, it teaches us how to transition from life hacks to "life back."

Brain Makeover (2019) by Phyllis Ginsberg. In this interactive book, you fill in a weekly journal for a year. Each week you reflect on and pen your thoughts on some aspect of your life. Week One begins with you listing your top three worries. For the next seven days in Week 2, you write your happiest moments of the day. Then, in subsequent weeks, one day at a time, you fight through your moments of hesitation on things you want to do, you choose to give the gift of your time to someone, you agree to receive a gift of time from someone. In Week 9, you clear out your drawer, one thing every day. In Week 13, you find someone to laugh with; in Week 22, you do a random act of kindness each day. In Week 25, you bring out your inner child: play a new sport; visit a zoo; do gardening; do photography; do puzzles; listen to different types of music; dance; try acting in a play; read a science book; etc., etc.

In Week 32, the book tells you to try to be one new you every day of the week: Be an athlete; be a healthy eater; be peace; be beauty, and so on.

In Week 52, make some brain-compatible New Year's resolutions; then imagine the experience of being successful at fulfilling those resolutions.

Very light prose, simple exercises, and once you immerse yourself into these, you cannot but feel the changed you, the new you.

Summarizing the above, I will shortlist for you three things you may wish to try:

1. Re-visualize your work so as to see meaning in it anew;
2. In your job and in social life alike, cultivate the habit of being interested in people; and
3. Identify one "monkey mind" habit a month and practice breaking free of it.

If you are reading this book, you are the type of person who enjoys watching what humans say and do. That outlook itself makes you a good candidate for living a more fulfilled life. I am excited to see you want to explore what a more meaningful life will be for you.

One More Time, What Should We Say to Them?

Okay, we now have only the last ten left. This idea of thinking about what we will say if we met these people is interesting. It gives us a reason to think deeper about our own ways of looking at life. Plus, it opens us to connecting with other people, human to human, no matter what their own outlook on life and on the world be.

So, let's continue.

If I met this person, this is what I will say to them:

(Memo to myself: I have to be nice!)

....

....

....

Listening Session 10
VOICES

91 92 93 94 95

96 97 98 99

100

I have much more appreciation for the simple things in life I look forward to. Like I'm craving going to a restaurant, sitting down and enjoying a meal. I never really realized how much I'd miss that but also shopping, just browsing in a store. Going forward, I'm going to be more careful but for the most part life goes on as normal.

I definitely won't be traveling out of country for at least the foreseeable future. I am going to be working more remotely too going forward as I really like it.

(Andrea, 31-40, high school, owner, $51-70, ND)

○ Sad   ○ Sour   ○ Sweet   ○ Soulful

I can relate to this *voice*:   ☐ A lot   ☐ Somewhat

This *voice* is opposite to
my own outlook: ☐ Somewhat   ☐ Totally

If I met this person, this is what I will say to them:
(Memo to myself: I have to be nice!)
....
....

We have a massive home improvement project currently going on,
all my free time went to progressing the project.

It's scary to know our freedoms can be taken from us so easily. I will likely get more involved in politics to ensure I have representatives that match my values.

Being more prepared for future situations like this, and likely more self-sustained.

(Cheyenne, 31-40, some college, accounting, $71-100K, AZ)

○ Sad   ○ Sour   ○ Sweet   ○ Soulful

I can relate to this *voice*:   ☐ A lot   ☐ Somewhat

This *voice* is opposite to
my own outlook: ☐ Somewhat   ☐ Totally

If I met this person, this is what I will say to them:
(Memo to myself: I have to be nice!)
....
....

Reading, additional bible study and more time talking to family/ friends.

Trump is more of a lying pro who is an incompetent moron.

Vote blue no matter who; get the lying moron out of office.

(George, 41-55, college degree, director, >$100K, NC)

○ Sad   ○ Sour   ○ Sweet   ○ Soulful

I can relate to this *voice*:   ☐ A lot   ☐ Somewhat

This *voice* is opposite to my own outlook: ☐ Somewhat   ☐ Totally

If I met this person, this is what I will say to them: (Memo to myself: I have to be nice!)

....

....

Spent time in the garden a lot, paying more attention to household chores, and doing research.

Stop trusting the democrats 100%!!! Seeing the democrats blame & attack President Trump for everything is disgusting. The democrats MUST be investigated for the Covid-19 virus.

No, I will not change anything. The democrats need to STOP their LYING about POTUS.

(Tucker, 56-65, some college, security, $51-70K, CO)

○ Sad   ○ Sour   ○ Sweet   ○ Soulful

I can relate to this *voice*: □ A lot   □ Somewhat

This *voice* is opposite to my own outlook: □ Somewhat   □ Totally

If I met this person, this is what I will say to them:
(Memo to myself: I have to be nice!)

···

···

Reading, Internet, phone calls, cleaning house, working at my hobbies that included gardening, photography, & coin collecting.

Because We Share a Nation

The previous two "voices" (#93 and #94) reflect the deep divide in America today and warrant our collective reflection. So, let me pause for a few moments here and speak to readers on each side of the divide.

This divide had been festering since the 2016 General Election with mutual political acrimony, but it intensified during the COVID-19 pandemic. The masking and lockdown mandates varied across the 50 states, as did the rates of infection, and public opinion coalesced at the opposite ends in blue and red states. This rift further widened with the arrival of the COVID-19 vaccine, as many a masking and lockdown protester joined the vaccine-opponent camp. Now the Twitterverse is replete with mutual diatribe and name-calling:

> @SteveCameronPr1 (July 28, 2021)
> *Provaxxers are like rabid dogs these days. Could it be their unsafe experimental Covid injections making them go bonkers?*

> @AkilahObviously (August 2, 2021)
> *Petition to call anti-vaxxers "plague rats!"*

Thus, pro-vaxxers and anti-vaxxers are spewing venom at each other. And this is no way to solve a problem, let alone survive as a prosperous and modern nation.

The root cause of the problem is the two entirely different belief sets: pro-vaxxers believe the vaccine to be their best insurance against threat to their health. In contrast, many anti-vaxxers believe the vaccine to be either unnecessary or ineffective, or worse, potentially causing adverse side-effects. If the consequences of these diverse belief sets were purely personal, perhaps the two sides could co-exist in harmony. But the pro-vaxxers believe that anti-vaxxers are in fact keeping the pandemic from being tamed, and worse, they are spreading infection (the Delta variant) even to the vaxxers. Therefore, they are angry at anti-vaxxers. Anti-vaxxers, in turn, resent any mandate to vaccinate or lock down.

How do we bridge this chasm? Derek Thomson, a staff writer at *The Atlantic*, shows one path. In one of his Twitter posts in May 2021, he invited anti-vaxxers to tell him why. He told them he was a staunch pro-vaxxer, but he assured them his goal was not to take them down; instead, he wanted to do an ethnography of their position. His respondents shared their reasons:

- Only approved for emergency use, therefore it is risky. It will have side-effects.

- I already got COVID so I now have antibodies and hence I do not need the vaccine.

- They have read that young people have a very low risk of getting the infection—lower than, say, car accidents.

- They instead believe in holistic, naturalistic, alternative medicine.

Thomson summarizes his discovery: "This is the no-vaxxers' deep story in a nutshell. *'I trust my own cells more than I trust pharmaceutical goop; I trust my own mind more than I trust liberal elites.'*"

Anti-anti-vaxxers think these views are "stupid." On the other side, anti-vaxxers think the vaxxers are the gullible ones who gave in to government propaganda.

I am fortunate to have friends on both sides. Although I am a pro-vaxxer, my anti-vaxxer friends have not yet abandoned me and I continue to enjoy their company. I can talk to each side with equal goodwill.

Let me speak first to my pro-vaxxer friends. As a pro-vaxxer, how would you behave toward the anti-vaxxers? Hold them in contempt? And then expect them to switch over to your side? A basic principle of persuasive communication psychology is that we cannot persuade anyone we hold in contempt. And our contempt will get communicated even if we try to overtly hide our feelings. You can't hide your disdain; and you can't fake goodwill. The trick then is to not feel any contempt to begin with. Or to rout out any contempt we may have hitherto harbored. To do this, we need a shot of empathy—we need to walk into their shoes. We need to do *ethnography*, Thompson style. *Ethnography* is the art of observing people in their cultural milieu, having a conversation with them to understand their belief system, and do so without judgment, with the objectivity of a scientist. Here is what we might discover.

First, not all of them are anti-vaxxers; or at least not vaccine-haters. Some of them are just *vaccine-hesitant* (In June 2021, according to a Kaiser Family Foundation survey, one-third of the unvaccinated were "wait and see"). *The New York Times* published a podcast ("the Daily") on August 7, 2021 ("Voices of the Unvaccinated") in which reporters Jan Hoffman and Sophie Kasakove spoke with the unvaxxed across the nation. That podcast features three of those interviews and deserves a listen by every pro-vaxxer. A larger selection of these voices was published in *the NYT* on July 31, 2021 (updated on August 4, 2021): "Who Are the Unvaccinated in America? There's No One Answer," by Julie Bosman, Jan Hoffman, Margot Sanger-Katz, and Tim Arango. Reading these accounts, I felt a good vibe toward their respondents. I wished I could hear their stories more. So, I wrote them short letters. I share them with you—this is how I believe pro-vaxxers and anti-vaxxers can be friends. (See Exhibit at the end of this note.)

Next, let me assume the role of an anti-vaxxer and speak to my anti-vaxxer friends—so, I am speaking to them here as if I am one of their own. Some of us indeed are *vaccine-opponents*, not just *vaccine-hesitants*. Consider our side of the story. We—the anti-vaxxers—have watched the political leaders we trust disparage vaccination or ridicule masking. We have been reminded, as well, of the sanctity of preserving our freedoms and resisting any action mandated on us by government agencies no matter how virtuous that act in itself be. We have also read news of some people getting the infection even after the vaccination, or of even dying, or of some people showing signs of a reaction. We hear these stories and we process raw data. As lay people we are not trained to ask scientific questions (and nor are you, dear pro-vaxxers). Therefore, we do not distinguish between episodic information (e.g., that five people got infected, or two people died) and "base rate" or "case rate" information (e.g., what proportion of the vaccinated got infected versus the proportion of the infected among the non-vaccinated, or what proportion of the vaccinated-and-infected died versus what proportion of those unvaccinated-and-infected died).

Some of us have been fed the information that Bill Gates is in cahoots with the government to inject a microchip along with the vaccine. Some of us have been told that the vaccine causes infertility. When health officials clarify that only one woman has been found to show this effect, the crowd screams out the contrary information we have been fed, "That is because you have hidden the news of thousands of other women." (There is no scientific evidence of this side-effect. And unvaccinated pregnant women are more at risk if they get infected with COVID-19.) Some of you (pro-vaxxers) believe that we (anti-vaxxers and anti-maskers) have been fed misinformation. In opposition, We believe you are the ones kept in the dark from the truth.

Let me now speak to both sides simultaneously. As pro-vaxxers, you are quick to pronounce anti-vaxxers irrational. But if you think about the information that their minds have had to process, purely from a communication theory point-of-view, their minds cannot but reach the conclusions they did reach. That that information could be false is a different matter. I am saying here only that when a mind is fed the information that it has been fed, it is rational and logical for that mind to reach the conclusions that are consistent with the input information. It is a basic function of the mind to work that way. It could be your mind or my mind.

Why have the minds of the anti-vaxxers been exposed to different information than the minds of the pro-vaxxers. That is because of our different places, families, social groups, communities, and cultures that we the pro- and the anti-vaxxers live in. And these same social and culture factors incline us to find certain sets of leaders and influencers credible and certain leaders and agencies and influencers despicable. That is why we follow the advice of the leaders we like. Just as you follow the advice of the leaders you like. Each of us is logical, faithfully marching to the tune we hear. Only, we hear two different tunes. We have a biased ear for our kind of tune. Just as you have a biased ear for the kind of tune that you like.

The spirit of my argument here is not to shift responsibility away from the individual to the environment. The argument does not speak to moral responsibility. It speaks to theory of communication and belief formation among individuals, groups, and whole communities. Our choices—those made in the present time but also those made from adolescence onward, much before the present crisis arrived—placed us in the midst of the social groups and cultures in which we now reside and from which we make sense of our lives and of things thrown at us. The pro-vaxxers among us are living everyday life in one set of social and cultural milieu; anti-vaxxers are living in another. Our culture and social groups define our identities. One group has no right to disdain the identity of the other group. Nothing is gained when pro-vaxers show contempt for anti-vaxxers. Nothing is gained when anti-vaxxers show disdain for pro-vaxxers.

The ethnographic interviews done by *the NYT* reporters Hoffman and Kasakove and the value-neutral listening sessions by Thomson (of *the Atlantic*) are models of how we should listen to each other. Such an exercise in ethnography makes us realize that had we been born and raised in the same place in the same social groups, we too might have acquired the mindset we now find foreign and despicable. That we acquired the opposite mindset of which we are proud is no reason to hold in contempt those who, with equal pride, harbor a different belief system. Nor do we need to adopt this posture of respect out of the goodness of our heart, although having a good heart definitely helps. We need to adopt this posture of respect simply to harness its *efficacy*. Without this posture of mutual respect, we cannot even begin to have a conversation, let alone persuade anyone.

I am in no delusion that with this posture of respect, persuasion will follow easily. I am sure only that with a posture of contempt and disrespect, persuasion has a zero chance of materializing. This goes both ways. With respectful interaction, each camp will at least begin to listen to the other side. We are the wrong agent to persuade any way. It is the same leaders and same influencers that they have hitherto been listening to who have to become the change agents. At the time of writing, while influential agents of anti-vaccine messaging persist, fortunately, some are changing their voice. Republican leaders like Senator Lindsey Graham, who got infected despite getting the vaccine, are expressing their conviction that for them, without the vaccine, the Delta variant infection would have been more deadly. Fox News began broadcasting a PSA: "America, we are in this together; so, if you can, get the vaccine" (I heard it on August 3, 2021). And in a rally of his followers in Alabama on August 21, 2021, former president Donald J. Trump began advising his followers to take the jab. So, going forward, there is reason for optimism.

For me, this ethnography stuff and adopting a posture of respect is not a mere theory. As I have proudly proclaimed before, among my friends are both pro-vaxxers and anti-vaxxers. They have shared with me their worldviews and revealed to me the solid evidential foundation of their beliefs—or the "misinformation" and "conspiratorial theories" as the other side calls this "evidence." My ethnographic mind does not allow me to judge. Call me naïve but I am thrilled to keep both camps as friends.

Republicans and Democrats. Pro-vaxxers and anti-vaxxers. Left-wing and Right-wing. Pro-science and science-skeptics. "Personal freedom above all" and "Community before personal freedom." Maskers and anti-maskers. Believers in government and those distrusting of it. No matter how irrational our ideologies, beliefs, and behaviors may look to each other, we share one common heritage: One nation. A modern, rational, and democratic nation. We can keep it only if we do not fight a war among ourselves.

Exhibit

My Letters to Our Vaccine-Hesitant Friends

Dear Alex, Steven, Myrna, Hanna, and Sherman:

I am so happy to meet you (courtesy of Jan Hoffman and Sophie Kasakove of *the NYT*). I must disclose: I am a pro-vaxxer, but I have friends on both sides and I enjoy powwowing with them on this vaccine issue. I want to chat with you a minute.

***

[Alex Garcia, 25: "I'm just trustworthy in my immune system, that since I'm young and healthy, my immune system could fight it."]

Dear Alex:

I see you in the photo, and yes, you do have a strong body. I am 90% sure, your system will fight it. I can't be 100% sure, though, and nor can you be.

The chances of us getting into a car accident are much less than 10%, but we still get the insurance. The chances of any of us tripping off and getting a small bone fracture that needs medical attention are less than 1 in a 1000, but we are not worried because we have health insurance.

As you know, there are two consequences of getting the infection: (1) We will fall sick, sometimes severely; and (2) we may not know we have it and unwittingly infect others— people not as lucky as us and who therefore do not have a strong immune system. In this process, we could spread the infection not just to one but five or ten people who are not as blessed with a strong immune system as we are. Yes, our own immune system will protect our bodies, but do we want to live the rest of our lives as persons who thought only about ourselves?

I do suppose you are not concerned about any immediate reaction and side effects, as your strong immune system will no doubt brace it with grace.

I'll see you on the other side soon.

148

[Steven Harris, 58, who believes that the antibodies he has from getting COVID-19 are sufficiently protective. "I heard news ... about the Epsilon variant.... So I don't want to get a vaccine now, and then get a different vaccine 9 months from now."]

Dear Steven:

The anti-bodies argument makes sense, but, still, I would ask my doctor. As to the Epsilon variant, here is how I look at it: If I get a cold and cough, I take an antihistamine; if it persists, my doctor prescribes antibiotics. We don't refuse to take antihistamine on the grounds that later we may have to take antibiotics anyway. Just a thought!

***

[Myrna Patterson, 85, a democrat from Rochester, N.Y., who works at a hospital. "Vaccines were produced too quickly" (implying they may not be safe or effective).]

Dear Myrna:

As of today (Aug 6), 153 million Americans have taken the vaccine (193 million one dose). No medicine on Earth is 100% effective or 100% safe—just read the label on a bottle of Tylenol or Aspirin or even Vitamin D!

***

[Hanna Reid: 30, a mother of four and a certified sommelier in Oregon. Apprehensive about vaccines. Her Christian faith has also made her comfortable with not yet getting a COVID-19 shot, which is too new (therefore unsafe).]

Dear Hanna:

About the newness of the vaccine, consider the fact that 193 million Americans have taken it; quite possibly, that is more than many other modern medicines. And does your Christian faith also not give you confidence that the vaccine will not have any adverse effects on you? Also, without being affected yourself, you could still pass on your infection to others, especially those who may not have the same faith and still resist vaccination for other reasons. The same Christian faith also teaches us to do something for other humans even if their faith is different from ours.

***

[Sherman Tillman, the president of the San Francisco Black Firefighter Association: "I don't believe that government should force our workers to do anything about their bodies and health. I think it is an individual choice."]

Dear Sherman:

First, I want to salute you for being a firefighter; people in your profession save lives, as do doctors and medicine makers. I agree with your "individual choice" idea. No government should force us to take a medicine for a headache, or treatment for a leg fracture, or force us to brush our teeth. And no government does. But if there is some part of my body or some action of my body that messes with other people's lives, I should expect to be asked (or even commanded) to restrain my body from doing that act of public nuisance. Suppose I wear a cologne and that cologne—my personal favorite—causes allergy to my coworkers; then I will just not wear that cologne. I could be self-centered but not that much!

Viruses have this evil mind: They use our otherwise noble bodies as carriers to spread themselves to our fellow humans—people we don't know but for whom we will endanger our own lives in our day jobs, such as in the job of a firefighter.

***

So, dear Alex, Steven, Myrna, Hanna, and Sherman: If you want to think these things over and decide to move to the other side, it is going to be your own decision. Your own free mind, following the logic. It was a pleasure chatting with you.

Ban Mittal   @BanMittal

Your Own Friendly Powwow

Okay, time for your own Powwow.

As a pro-vaxxer:

_____

_____

As an anti-vaxxer:

_____

_____

On either side: what will be your approach to keep the "voices" of both sides friendly?

_____

_____

Listening Session 10 (resume)
V O I C E S

95 **96** **97** **98** **99**

100

I have a new respect for people who put their own lives at risk to help others. I will appreciate things a lot more and not take even the small things for granted.

I will be taking better care of myself and those around me.

(José, 41-55, some college, unemployed, $10-30K, CA)

○ Sad   ○ Sour   ○ Sweet   ○ Soulful

I can relate to this *voice*:   ☐ A lot   ☐ Somewhat

This *voice* is opposite to
my own outlook: ☐ Somewhat   ☐ Totally

If I met this person, this is what I will say to them:
(Memo to myself: I have to be nice!)
....
....

I have been spending my extra time playing games, reading, walking more.

I will be more concerned about my health, I would have to treat people with respect, I would try to spend more time with family and friends, I would make better use of my time and I will attend more religious activities.

I would stop drinking alcohol, I know it won't be easy. I have started reducing my intake of alcohol and I know it's a gradual process, before the end of this year I think I would have stopped taking alcohol because it is not really good for the body.

(Dustin, 31-40, master's, technical manager, >$101K, CA)

○ Sad   ○ Sour   ○ Sweet   ○ Soulful

I can relate to this *voice*:	☐ A lot	☐ Somewhat
This *voice* is opposite to my own outlook:	☐ Somewhat	☐ Totally

If I met this person, this is what I will say to them:
(Memo to myself: I have to be nice!)
....

....

Watching movies, playing video games, cooking, listening to music, playing with family, dancing, reading books and novels and some other things, I have also spent more time on social media chatting with people, looking at different posts and I have also been praying.

No. Our government made healthy people pris-
oners. We should not lock up the healthy because then this is tyranny.

Yes, go to church in spite of what the government said.

(Beth, 41-55, college degree, teacher assistant, $31-50K, NV)

○ Sad   ○ Sour   ○ Sweet   ○ Soulful

I can relate to this *voice*:	☐ A lot	☐ Somewhat
This *voice* is opposite to my own outlook:	☐ Somewhat	☐ Totally

If I met this person, this is what I will say to them:
(Memo to myself: I have to be nice!)

....

....

Free time was for making masks and making most of our food from scratch. No time for free time.

I need to be more prepared and I have much less faith in the human race that's for sure. We all are going to die 100% of life and in death, so too many stupid people on this Earth that don't do what they're supposed to do so maybe they deserve to die this is crazy.

Absolutely, because this has changed everything about the World As We Know It is it going to be a colder place than it was before; will become more divided because we have to socially distance; we can't really be social so it's going to really suck.

(Melanie, 31-40, master's, small biz owner, $71-100K, NV)

○ Sad   ○ Sour   ○ Sweet   ○ Soulful

| I can relate to this *voice*: | ☐ A lot | ☐ Somewhat |
| This *voice* is opposite to my own outlook: | ☐ Somewhat | ☐ Totally |

If I met this person, this is what I will say to them:
(Memo to myself: I have to be nice!)

....

....

I adopted a dog I got organized, did a lot of DIY projects too.

I do not feel my overall perspective on life will change. However, I do believe my perspective has/will change with regards to large American companies, and how they have protected/not protected their font-line employees. Furthermore, I've grown disappointed with the lack of regard from my fellow Americans (not all, of course) who do not abide by stay-at-home orders, and continue to be negligent to orders from medical professionals, etc., to stay at home, unless absolutely necessary.

(Charlie, 31-40, college degree, asst. manager, $31-45K, KY)

○ Sad   ○ Sour   ○ Sweet   ○ Soulful

I can relate to this *voice*: ☐ A lot   ☐ Somewhat

This *voice* is opposite to my own outlook: ☐ Somewhat   ☐ Totally

If I met this person, this is what I will say to them: (Memo to myself: I have to be nice!)

....

....

I have not engaged in any new activities during the Coronavirus. However, I have been spending more time outside with my family (playing, taking bike rides, having bonfires, walking the dogs, etc.).

History always repeats itself. We live and we learn, and we cannot let this affect how we live our daily lives.

We must make proper preparation to overcome future problems personally and as a society. Life goes on.

(Arch, 31-40, college degree, retail, $60-100K, OH)

○ Sad   ○ Sour   ○ Sweet   ○ Soulful

I can relate to this *voice*:	☐ A lot	☐ Somewhat
This *voice* is opposite to my own outlook:	☐ Somewhat	☐ Totally

If I met this person, this is what I will say to them:
(Memo to myself: I have to be nice!)

....

....

I worked as usual.

Overview Session 11

VOICES
REVISITED

Worth Re-Listening?

This is actually a re-listening session. Let's go back to all of the answers. Not all of them at once, of course. But over several days.

We can simply re-listen to them selectively and see if we want to re-assign them to a different group. And then we can cull them together all on a single page, using a 4x4 crosstab shown on the following page.

Do you see a pattern in this crosstab? Do the voices fall more in one cell, less in other cells? Do you see yourself relating to one type (e.g., 'sad' or 'sweet') more? If yes, ask yourself why.

Finally, "speak" your own voice. How has your voice been affected by your listening to all these voices in this book?

CROSSTAB

How I Relate to These Voices

	Relate totally	Relate somewhat	Somewhat opposite	Totally opposite
Sad				
Sour				
Sweet				
Soulful				

① ② ③ ④ ⑤ ⑥ ⑦ ⑧ ⑨ ⑩
⑪ ⑫ ⑬ ⑭ ⑮ ⑯ ⑰ ⑱ ⑲ ⑳
㉑ ㉒ ㉓ ㉔ ㉕ ㉖ ㉗ ㉘ ㉙ ㉚
㉛ ㉜ ㉝ ㉞ ㉟ ㊱ ㊲ ㊳ ㊴ ㊵
㊶ ㊷ ㊸ ㊹ ㊺ ㊻ ㊼ ㊽ ㊾ ㊿
51 52 53 54 55 56 57 58 59 60
61 62 63 64 65 66 67 68 69 70
71 72 73 74 75 76 77 78 79 80
81 82 83 84 85 86 87 88 89 90
91 92 93 94 95 96 97 98 99 100

Write these numbers in the cells of the CROSSTAB above.

My Own Voice:

The activities I did during the lockdown:

Here is my new perspective:

Going forward, this is how I will live my life:

This is how this book affected my own "voice":

....

....

....

Epilogue

I did this survey in May 2020, right in the midst of the lockdown. It paints a picture of how people felt as they were learning to practice the virus safety regimen and managing everyday life without being able to go out. We will remember both the pandemic and the lockdown for a long time to come.

Some of you may have read about previous pandemics. The Black Death pandemic occurred from 1346 to 1353 and killed an estimated 75 to 200 million people. The Spanish flu, the last pandemic, occurred during 1918-1920 and killed an estimated 50 million or more people worldwide. We can read about the devastation these pandemics caused in history books. But how people at large (infected or not) felt, we will never know.

If 5 or 10 years later, when our five-year-old children will have grown up and ask, or 10 or 20 or 30 years later, the new generation of 10- or 20- or 30-year-olds, not yet born, ask what COVID-19 pandemic was like, give them some history books to read. Those books will tell them that COVID-19 had killed 4.30 million people worldwide (as of August 8, 2021). Help them visualize that number. That number is as large as the population of Oregon. Or about half the population of London (UK). Beyond the numbers, to give them a feel for the human experience, give them this book to read.

We are not out of the woods yet. On June 28, 2021, Australia declared a new lockdown to contain the Delta variant. The vaccination rate there had been only 15%. And on July 28,

2021, the U.S. Centers for Disease Control and Prevention (CDC) issued new guidelines, recommending wearing masks indoors, even if vaccinated. Similar calls for masking and vaccination have been issued with renewed urgency in Europe and in countries across the world.

For all its misery, the lockdown did have a silver lining: It forced us to rearrange everyday life. For some of us, the chores of living increased. For some, there was more free time, and we found new creative ways of filling that time. In my own research, I found that people who spent their time in new productive and creative work (e.g., new hobbies, gardening, arts and crafts, or even DIY projects) or led more active lives felt less anxiety than those who spent their time in passive entertainment (e.g., TV and video) or just idling. If you re-listen to some of the 100 voices closely, you will see a glimpse of this pattern. Yes, it helps to find a new hobby, a new passion—where our bodies get exercised and our minds get creative.

In my research, I have also found that the pandemic made many people feel greater altruism or generosity—a desire to do something good for their communities. According to a Gates Foundation report, 56 percent of US households gave to charity or volunteered in response to the pandemic, with a 12.6% increase in new donors. And Charity Navigator (a tracker) reported that donations to Feeding America increased 1,980 percent year over year, and donations to Doctors Without Borders increased 131 percent year over year. I call this the "rise of a 'virtuous mind.'" Glance back through all the voices you marked "soulful" and see if you don't notice the rise of this virtue in many of the voices.

The lockdown gave us a taste of a life different from what we had lived our entire time on Earth. Whether we felt that taste as sad, sour, sweet, or soulful, it showed us new possibilities. New responsibilities. New opportunities. It made us think differently.

Those of us who felt the "sad" or "sour" taste in our own lives, let us use the voices of the "sweet" and the "soulful" types to feel the silver lining. Let us feel those same perspectives vicariously. After all, we don't want to live with that sadness, and we don't want to keep that sour taste in our mouths for the rest of our lives. The "sweet" and the "soulfuls" were face-to-face with the same pandemic and the same lockdown as we were, and yet they were able to see a silver lining; we too want to taste the same "nectar of life." We want to look at life and the world through the same lenses of positivity.

On the other hand, if we are the "sweet" or "soulful" types, let us harness our positivity to understand the inner struggles of the "sad" and the "sour." They had their reasons. Let us hope someday soon they will be able to come out of their current outlook of "sad" and "sour." Let us help them in that transition.

We now have the vaccine, made possible by the resolute dedication of our former president, who marshaled all resources into harnessing the drug R&D companies. Science has come to our rescue. And the vaccine is available in every town and every village in the USA (and in much of the world), thanks to our current president's resolve to bring it to the doorsteps of every American. Americans are getting the vaccine in droves (65% at the time of writing had received at least one dose) because they believe it is the strongest self-protection one could ever hope for—99.5% of the deaths during the 6 months of January to June, 2021, occurred among the non-vaccinated! Or because they consider protecting others their civil duty, an act of patriotism. Let us welcome more and more people into the fold, the "sad" or the "sour" types and the "sweet" and the "soulful" types alike. Many will do it—take the vaccine—ultimately because they recognize that it is their patriotic duty. And in displaying patriotism, we Americans are second to none. Nor are the British, the Germans, the Brazilians, the Italians, or the Indians. Our patriotism, the patriotism of each of the four types, gives us hope the world will soon emerge out of the pandemic and out of the new lockdowns.

We—the "sweet" and "soulful" types among us—what are we going to do for ourselves? Let us cultivate those good feelings even more. It is a law of nature that time makes us forget. As the economy reopens, let us flock to the open world, to the marketplace, of course, to soak in the wonderful experiences we had once taken for granted. But with equal zeal, let us nurture our "sweet" and our "soulful" perspectives as well. Let us act on our newfound wisdom to pursue a greater work-life balance. Let us make our work more meaningful.

The "voices" in the book are just that—voices! They echo our feelings at the moment. Individually, they do not necessarily represent our complete selves. We are, at the moment, experiencing a catastrophe of a lifetime. We could not have imagined that a disease that is so invisible that the infected do not show symptoms for days and weeks could invade our world;

that we could get it from friends and family members and strangers alike; that it will forbid us to touch things, surfaces, pets, people; that we will lose the freedom to go to places to eat, shop, worship, and mingle; that we will be ordered to stay within the bounds of our homes. And face the possibility that we could still get the disease, and that if we got it, there may not be a hospital bed available to us. We experienced this period of catastrophe variously: for some of us, rearranging our work and personal lives became a hassle, even a nightmare; for some of us, more time at home became a blessing in disguise. The "voices" reflect this varied experience.

No matter what be the tone of our "voice" in this moment, each of us in our persona at large harbors a tinge of each tone. Each of us is therefore capable of cultivating the "sweet" and the "soulful" sides of our being. With near-universal adoption of the vaccine, we will soon tame COVID-19 and its Delta variant for good. Soon we will be fully free of the lockdown. Each of us can emerge with a "sweet" and a "soulful" voice.

The *Sad*, the *Sour*, the *Sweet*, and the *Soulful*, let each of us use this once-in-a-lifetime experience to take action to improve our material, family, social and spiritual life. And if we haven't asked already, let us ask as well, *how to make our life more purposeful, more meaningful.* For ourselves and for the world we live in!

MOVING FORWARD

A Manifesto

A Sane Person's Guide For COVID Times

1 As a pro-masker, I will understand that some people may have genuine breathing problems with a mask. They do not necessarily oppose the mask and they do not secretly hold me in derision for wearing it.

2 As a pro-vaxxer, I will understand that some people may have genuine health factors that lead them to view the vaccine risky to their personal health. I should not assume they are not cool with my having had the vaccine.

3 As a pro-vaxxer, I will understand that people who oppose the vaccine are guided by their belief system. They have the right to hold those beliefs even if I disagree with those beliefs; I must respect them as independent-minded persons, nonetheless.

4 As an anti-masker, I will understand that I am free to not wear a mask when: a. I am alone by myself; b. I am in my own house; and c. when I am with friends and family members in a private residence or in open public spaces. I understand that strangers have the right to keep social distance from the unmasked me.

5 I understand that it is the right of a business establishment to set all policies related to how customers should behave inside their premises, as long as any restrictions they impose are allowed by the law of our land. The same law of the land does not condone my disrespecting other customers who may comply with those restrictions.

6 Whoever be my opinion leaders that I follow, I will expect them to publicly declare their vaccination status. I respect their argument that it is one's personal matter. But if they choose to opine on vaccine, then it is not their private matter anymore, because if I follow their opinion, it affects my personal health and well-being. I must also consider that celebrities have privileged access to premium medical services that I may not have.

7. When a media celebrity or a politician offers an opinion, I must ask, is there a personal benefit motive for this person to broadcast that opinion. For example, they might try to echo my beliefs just to please me and manipulate me into giving them my "like" and my patronage. I must know that social media influencers do not know me and therefore will not know what is good for me; their main goal is to get a large following by spreading sensational ideology.

8. I am not gullible if an anti-vaxxer friend were trying to persuade me. I am not gullible if a pro-vaxxer friend were trying to persuade me. Likewise, when a media celebrity with no subject matter expertise and having a personal agenda expresses an opinion, no matter which side that opinion is on, I should not be gullible.

9. Whether I am a pro- or anti-masker and whether I am a pro- or anti-vaxxer, rather than believing just what I hear or read on social media, I will try to get the facts behind the effects of masking and the effects of vaccine; I will try to learn from independent expert sources that have no ambition of gaining a large number of followers. I should also try to learn for myself the trends in infections, overcrowding in hospitals, and COVID-deaths, and I must try to do my part in mitigating these sufferings in others by not aiding the pandemic to spread.

10. Before the pandemic came, we got along well. Now, we are doing what we can to overcome the pandemic. The COVID's toll on our fellow citizens is sad enough. We will not allow the pandemic to also ruin our relations among ourselves, pitting us on opposite sides. No matter which side of the lockdown, masking, and vaccine we find ourselves, we shall not harbor disrespect and ill will toward the other side. We want to guard, naturally, our right to be respected. With equal zeal, we will guard the right of the opposite side to be respected. No matter which leader we follow, this is the God's *Golden Rule*!

RESOURCES FOR MAKING EDUCATED DECISIONS

About the Covid-19 Vaccine

(1) **Johns Hopkins Medicine**
Covid-19 Story Tip: Five Things You May Not Know About Vaccine Science
12/15/2020
https://tinyurl.com/Voice-Vaxx-1
Also a Video:
https://tinyurl.com/Voice-Vaxx-Video-1

Video

(2) **The Ohio State University, Wexner Medical Center**
"The COVID-19 vaccine is safe and effective"
How do we know this? Because our experts have dedicated their lives to studying how infectious diseases and vaccines work. While the COVID-19 vaccines are new, the technology they use has been studied and refined for decades.
https://tinyurl.com/Voice-Vaxx-2

COVID-19 vaccine side effects: Should we be concerned? How does mRNA work?
Carlos Malvestutto, MD, MPH
https://tinyurl.com/Voice-Vaxx-3

(3) **The Pew Charitable Trust**
The Science Behind Vaccines
Two Pew biomedical researchers answer common questions
March 5, 2021
https://tinyurl.com/Voice-Vaxx-4

(4) **CDC**
Understanding How COVID-19 Vaccines Work
Updated May 27, 2021
https://tinyurl.com/Voice-Vaxx-5

(5) **The New York Times**
letter 197
As a Doctor, I Was Skeptical About the Covid Vaccine. Then I Reviewed the Science.
How one emergency department doctor shifted her views.
By Amaali Lokuge (M.D. at Royal Melbourne Hospital)
March 4, 2021
https://tinyurl.com/Voice-Vaxx-6

(6) **Business Insider**
The COVID-19 vaccine side-effects you can expect based on your age, sex, and dose
Aria Bendix (Mar 30, 2021)
https://tinyurl.com/Voice-Vaxx-7

(7) **Johns Hopkins**
How Do We Know a COVID-19 Vaccine Will Be Safe and Effective? (Dec 3, 2020)
https://tinyurl.com/Voice-Vaxx-Video-1 (1:06)

Video

(8) **American Medical Association**
How to defeat COVID-19 vaccine misinformation with facts, science
Len Strazewski, Jun 4, 2021
https://tinyurl.com/Voice-Vaxx-Video-2 (56:12)

Video

(9) **Science Magazine**
How do the leading COVID-19 vaccines work? Science explains
By Meagan Cantwell, Jan. 29, 2021
https://tinyurl.com/Voice-Vaxx-Video-3 (4:43)

Video

(10) **Texas Public Radio**
Think Science: How Vaccines Work
By Nathan Cone (May 14, 2020)
https://tinyurl.com/Voice-Vaxx-Video-4 (58:50)

Video

(11) **Union of Concerned Scientists**
Frequently Asked Questions about the COVID-19 Vaccine
Apr 2, 2021
https://tinyurl.com/Voice-Vaxx-Video-5 (3:33)

Video

(12) **PBS.org**
Vaccines against the coronavirus will have side effects – and that's a good thing (Dec 3, 2020)
https://tinyurl.com/Voice-Vaxx-Video-6 (1:47)

Video

(13) **TheConversation.com**
New COVID-19 vaccine warnings don't mean it's unsafe – they mean the system to report side effects is working
July 19, 2021
https://tinyurl.com/Voice-Vaxx-Video-7 (10:55)

Video

About Masks

(14) University of California San Francisco
Still Confused About Masks? Here's the Science Behind How Face Masks Prevent Coronavirus
By Nina Bai, June 26, 2020
https://tinyurl.com/Voice-Mask-1

(15) National Jewish Hospital
The Science Behind the Mask
Includes very helpful infographics
https://tinyurl.com/Voice-Mask-2

(16) FactCheck.org
The Evolving Science of Face Masks and COVID-19
By Jessica McDonald
March 2, 2021
https://tinyurl.com/Voice-Mask-3

(17) Science Magazine
Face masks effectively limit the probability of SARS-CoV-2 transmission
Science, 25 Jun 2021:
Vol. 372, Issue 6549, pp. 1439-1443
https://tinyurl.com/Voice-Mask-5

(18) PNAS Journal
An evidence review of face masks against COVID-19
January 26, 2021 118 (4) e2014564118;
https://tinyurl.com/Voice-Mask-6

(19) Nature (magazine)
Face masks: what the data say
Lynne Peeples (October 6, 2020)
https://tinyurl.com/Voice-Mask-7

20 **NBC Nightly News**
How Scientists Test Face Mask Effectiveness Against Corona-virus
Jun 21, 2020
https://tinyurl.com/Voice-Mask-Video-1 (2:03)

Video

21 **FOX NEWS**
Scientific evidence for mask wearing
May 22, 2020
Dr. John Campbell
https://tinyurl.com/Voice-Mask-Video-2 (22:00)

Video

22 **University of California San Francisco**
Still Confused About Masks? Here's the Science Behind How Face Masks Prevent Coronavirus
By Nina Bai, June 26, 2020
https://tinyurl.com/Voice-Mask-Video-3 (5:01)

Video

23 **NPR.org**
Yes, Wearing Masks Helps. Here's Why - NPR
Mary Godoy (6/21/2020)
https://tinyurl.com/Voice-Mask-Video-4 (3:29)

Video

24 **CNN.Com**
School openings so far reveal science is right – masking works
By Jacqueline Howard, CNN
August 12, 2021
https://tinyurl.com/Voice-Mask-Video-5 (1:31)

Video

On Social Distancing

(25) **Johns Hopkins University**
Coronavirus, Social and Physical Distancing and Self-Quarantine
Lisa Lockerd Maragakis, M.D., M.P.H.
https://tinyurl.com/Voice-SocDist-1

(26) **HealthyChildren.org**
COVID-19: Keep On Keeping Your Distance
By Corinn Cross, MD, FAAP
https://tinyurl.com/Voice-SocDist-2

(27) **Jackson Laboratory**
What is the science behind the social distancing recommendations?
March 26, 2020
Edison Liu, Jill Goldthwait
https://tinyurl.com/Voice-SocDist-3

(28) **AARP**
Social Distancing: What It Is, Why It's Important, How to Do It
It's not the same as a quarantine, and it's not just for high-risk populations
by Rachel Nania, *AARP*, April 13, 2020
https://tinyurl.com/Voice-SocDist-4

(29) **The Conversation**
Why social distancing is one of the best tools we have to fight the coronavirus
Thomas Perls, Professor of Medicine at Boston University.
https://tinyurl.com/Voice-SocDist-Video-1 (2:18)

Video

(30) **Mayo Clinic**
COVID-19: Why social distancing, having a personal plan is important
Deb Balzer
March 13, 2020
https://tinyurl.com/Voice-SocDist-Video-2 (2:00)

Video

Endnotes

Preface:

"Governor Gavin Newsom Issues Stay at Home Order," Mar 19, 2020, Office of the Governor, California. https://www.gov.ca.gov/2020/03/19/governor-gavin-newsom-issues-stay-at-home-order/ (DOA: Aug. 16, 2021).

"Australia tightens lockdown amid Delta virus outbreak, vaccine chaos," *Reuters*, June 29, 2021.

"Interim Public Health Recommendations for Fully Vaccinated People," CDC, July 28, 2021. https://www.cdc.gov/coronavirus/2019-ncov/vaccines/fully-vaccinated-guidance.html (DOA: Aug. 16, 2021).

Meaning of Soulful:

Cambridge English Dictionary.

My conversation with Patricia

Data on infections and death in Pennsylvania: https://www.health.pa.gov/topics/disease/coronavirus/Pages/Cases.aspx (DOA: Aug 16, 2021).

Sturgis Rally: "COVID-19 Outbreak Associated with a 10-Day Motorcycle Rally in a Neighboring State—Minnesota, August–September 2020," *CDC*, Weekly / November 27, 2020 / 69(47);1771-1776. https://www.cdc.gov/mmwr/volumes/69/wr/mm6947e1.htm (DOA: Aug. 16, 2021).

Access to water: "663 Million Children Lack Access to Basic Human Rights Like Clean Water," *Global Citizen*, July 12, 2019. https://www.globalcitizen.org/en/content/multidimensional-poverty-un/ (DOA: Aug, 16, 2021).

Sorry to Interrupt: Dear Josh

"9 Famous Beauties that Used to be Ugly Ducklings and Became Idols for Millions," https://brightside.me/wonder-people/9-famous-beauties-that-used-to-be-ugly-ducklings-and-became-idols-for-millions-788610/ (DOA: Aug. 16, 2021).

Because We Share A Nation

"Millions Are Saying No to the Vaccines. What Are They Thinking?," By Derek Thompson, *The Atlantic*, May 3, 2021. https://www.theatlantic.com/ideas/archive/2021/05/the-people-who-wont-get-the-vaccine/618765/ (DOA: Aug. 16, 2021).

"Voices of the Unvaccinated," Daily (podcast), *The New York Times*, Aug. 6, 2021. https://www.nytimes.com/2021/08/06/podcasts/the-daily/delta-variant-coronavirus-vaccine.html (DOA: Aug 16, 2021).

"Vaccine Monitor: Some Who Were Hesitant to Get a Vaccine in January Say They Changed Their Mind Because of Family, Friends and Their Personal Doctors," *KFF*, July 13, 2021. https://www.kff.org/coronavirus-covid-19/press-release/vaccine-monitor-some-who-were-hesitant-to-get-a-vaccine-in-january-say-they-changed-their-mind-because-of-family-friends-and-their-personal-doctors/ (DOA: Aug 16, 2021).

"Here's Where That COVID-19 Vaccine Infertility Myth Came From — And Why It Is Not True," *Henry Ford Health System,* April 23, 2021. https://www.henryford.com/blog/2021/04/fertility-rumor-covid-vaccine (DOA: Aug. 16, 2021).

Epilogue

"The Black Death: The Greatest Catastrophe Ever," Ole Benedictow, *History Today*, Vol.55 (3), March 2005. https://www.historytoday.com/archive/black-death-greatest-catastrophe-ever (DOA: Aug 16, 2021).

"The 1918 Flu Pandemic Was Brutal, Killing More Than 50 Million People Worldwide," *NPR*, April 2, 2020. https://www.npr.org/2020/04/02/826358104/the-1918-flu-pandemic-was-brutal-killing-as-many-as-100-million-people-worldwide (DOA: Aug. 16, 2021).

"U.S. COVID Deaths Are Rising Again. Experts Call It A 'Pandemic of The Unvaccinated'," *NPR*, July 16, 2021. https://www.npr.org/2021/07/16/1017002907/u-s-covid-deaths-are-rising-again-experts-call-it-a-pandemic-of-the-unvaccinated. (DOA: Aug. 16, 2021).

Vox (2021), "Covid-19 Pandemic: Generosity, Charity," *Vox magazine.* https://www.vox.com/future-perfect/21754625/covid-19-pandemic-generosity-charity-cash-transfers. (DOA Aug 16, 2021).

About the Author

Ban Mittal is a social scientist with a Ph.D. in consumer psychology from the University of Pittsburgh. He has been a professor of marketing at SUNY (Buffalo), University of Miami (FL), UNSW (Australia), and at Northern Kentucky University, where he currently teaches marketing and consumer behavior and researches how humans pursue happiness in the world of goods.

He is the author of *ValueSpace* (2001), *Consumer Psychology: A Modernistic Explanation* (2021), *50 Faces of Happy* (2020), and *My Uber Story* (2020). He lives in Cincinnati, Ohio.

TW: @BanMittal.com   IG: Happy2Me2020
YT: tinyurl.com/BanMittal-YT   www.BanMittal.com